A 31-Day Devotional
Journey Through
Proverbs 31

IN HER IMAGE

ANDREA JOHN

Copyright © 2025 by Andrea John
In Her Image: A 31-Day Devotional Journey Through Proverbs 31

All rights reserved. No portion of this book may be reproduced, stored in a retrieval system, or transmitted in any form or by any means—electronic, mechanical, photocopy, recording, scanning, or otherwise—except for brief quotations in critical reviews or articles, without the prior written permission of the publisher.

ISBN (Softcover): 978-1-0685770-6-2
ISBN (Hardcover): 978-1-0685770-7-9

Published by Paper Crown Media
www.papercrownmedia.com

Cover by Meliza Farndell
Interior design and format: Andrea John
Formatted by Paper Crown Media

Scripture quotations taken from the Holy Bible, New International Version®, NIV®.
Copyright © 1973, 1978, 1984, 2011 by Biblica, Inc.™
Used by permission. All rights reserved worldwide.
www.zondervan.com
The "NIV" and "New International Version" are trademarks registered in the United States Patent and Trademark Office by Biblica, Inc.™

TABLE OF CONTENTS

From My Heart to Yours

How to Use The Devotional

Proverbs 31

1	Wise Counselor	1
2	Focus	7
3	Advocate	13
4	Just	19
5	Noble	25
6	Trustworthy	31
7	Goodness	37
8	Wholehearted	43
9	Diligent	49
10	Excellent	55
11	Responsible	61
12	Visionary	67
13	Resilient	73
14	Purposeful	79
15	Skillful	85
16	Generous	91

17	Kind	97
18	Proactive	103
19	Caring	109
20	Integrity	115
21	Driven	121
22	Dignified	127
23	Hopeful	133
24	Wise	139
25	Intentional	145
26	Attentive	151
27	Legacy	157
28	Exceptional	163
29	Devoted	169
30	Humble	175
31	Honorable	181
	About the Author	
	Paper Crown Media	

From My Heart to Yours

If you've ever felt like you were trying to live up to a version of womanhood that didn't quite fit, this devotional is for you.

For most of my life, I struggled with identity. I didn't know who I was, and honestly, I didn't feel like I could be who I was, even if I had known. Life had shaped me, expectations had boxed me in, and I carried a quiet ache to know who I was beyond what I did. Maybe you've been there too.

Everything changed when I started learning more about who God is—not just the surface-level knowledge of His existence, but the deeper truths of His character. The more I discovered about His nature—His love, light, creativity, justice, and fatherhood—the more I saw myself clearly. I began to understand that I was created in His image. And if I wanted to understand who I was, I had to start with who He is.

That journey led me to write a book called In His Image, where I explore the five foundational attributes of God: Love, Light, Creator, Father, and Judge. These five truths have become anchors in my life, and they are the lens through which I now view myself and the world around me.

So naturally, when I returned to Proverbs 31, I saw it with new eyes.

I've always loved the book of Proverbs. For years, I made it a personal rhythm to read through the entire book at least once a year, letting its wisdom shape my choices, sharpen my discernment, and center my heart on what matters most. But one year, something shifted. I found myself returning to Proverbs 31, not just as the closing chapter of a book I'd read many times before, but as an invitation to go deeper.

That year, I didn't move on after reading it once. I stayed. I sat with that chapter for an entire month, reading it slowly, line by line, letting each verse speak to me. I had read it dozens of times, but this time I wasn't reading it to check off a box. I was reading it to understand her.

The more I sat with it, the more I realized that the Proverbs 31 woman isn't defined by what she does. She's defined by who she is.

So often, when people teach or talk about Proverbs 31, the focus is on her actions—sewing, buying fields, rising early, selling garments—and for many of us, those examples feel disconnected from our modern lives. When we look deeper, past the surface of her responsibilities, we see something far more important: her character.

That's what this devotional is about. It's not a to-do list. It's an invitation to become the woman God designed you to be. Each day, we'll reflect on one character trait revealed in the Proverbs 31 woman, thirty-one traits that reflect her strength, purpose, and identity, and ultimately, the image of the God she serves.

Whether you're reading this as a mom, wife, daughter, leader, student, or friend, know this: You are made in His image. When you learn who He is, you'll discover who you are.

Let this devotional be a journey of rediscovery, a chance to shed the pressure of perfection and step into the beauty of becoming who you were always created to be.

You don't have to become her overnight. You just have to start with today.

With much love,

Andrea

How To Use The Devotional

This devotional is designed to take you on a 31-day journey through Proverbs 31, focusing on the character of the woman described in that passage. Each day highlights one trait reflected in her life. These traits are just as relevant for us today as they were then.

You'll notice a familiar rhythm each day with these five sections:

IN HER WALK
This is the devotional heart of the day. Here you'll read a thoughtful reflection rooted in Scripture that explores the character trait of the woman described in Proverbs 31. This section is meant to encourage, challenge, and inspire you as you walk out your own journey of faith, purpose, and identity.

IN HIS IMAGE
This section shows how the day's character trait reflects an attribute of God Himself. As women made in God's image, we are invited to grow into His likeness—not through striving, but through intimacy. This part of the devotional is tied to my book In His Image: Discover Your True Identity, where we explore the nature of God as Father, Creator, Love, Light, and Judge. Each day's reflection points back to who He is and who we are because of it.

THINK ABOUT IT
These two journal prompts provide space for you to reflect on what you've read. They're designed to help you pause, listen, and write from a place of authenticity and openness. Write directly in the book or grab a journal, take your time, and revisit these questions often.

LIVE THIS TODAY
Every trait is only as powerful as our willingness to apply it. This section offers a specific, practical way for you to activate what you've learned. You'll be prompted to respond—to plan, write, pray, or take action—in a way that helps solidify your growth and make it personal.

DAILY FOCUS
Each day includes a short, one-sentence phrase you can carry with you. It's a truth to remember, speak aloud, or meditate on as you go about your day. It's your daily anchor.

EXTRA NOTES
You'll also find a blank, lined page for additional notes, reflections, or prayers. Use it however you'd like. This is your space.

PROVERBS 31

The sayings of King Lemuel contain this message, which his mother taught him.

O my son, O son of my womb,
O son of my vows,
do not waste your strength on women,
on those who ruin kings.

It is not for kings, O Lemuel, to guzzle wine.
Rulers should not crave alcohol.
For if they drink, they may forget the law
and not give justice to the oppressed.
Alcohol is for the dying,
and wine for those in bitter distress.
Let them drink to forget their poverty
and remember their troubles no more.

Speak up for those who cannot speak for themselves;
ensure justice for those being crushed.
Yes, speak up for the poor and helpless,
and see that they get justice.
A Wife of Noble Character
Who can find a virtuous and capable wife?
She is more precious than rubies.

Her husband can trust her,
and she will greatly enrich his life.
She brings him good, not harm,
all the days of her life.

She finds wool and flax
and busily spins it.
She is like a merchant's ship,
bringing her food from afar.
She gets up before dawn to prepare breakfast for her household
and plan the day's work for her servant girls.

She goes to inspect a field and buys it;
with her earnings she plants a vineyard.
She is energetic and strong,
a hard worker.
She makes sure her dealings are profitable;
her lamp burns late into the night.

Her hands are busy spinning thread,
her fingers twisting fiber.
She extends a helping hand to the poor
and opens her arms to the needy.
She has no fear of winter for her household,
for everyone has warm clothes.

She makes her own bedspreads.
She dresses in fine linen and purple gowns.
Her husband is well known at the city gates,
where he sits with the other civic leaders.
She makes belted linen garments
and sashes to sell to the merchants.

She is clothed with strength and dignity,
and she laughs without fear of the future.
When she speaks, her words are wise,
and she gives instructions with kindness.
She carefully watches everything in her household
and suffers nothing from laziness.

Her children stand and bless her.
Her husband praises her:
"There are many virtuous and capable women in the world,
but you surpass them all!"

Charm is deceptive, and beauty does not last;
but a woman who fears the Lord will be greatly praised.
Reward her for all she has done.
Let her deeds publicly declare her praise.

WISE COUNSELOR

The sayings of King Lemuel—an inspired utterance his mother taught him.

Proverbs 31:1

IN HER WALK

The opening verse of Proverbs 31 introduces us to King Lemuel, a man shaped by the wisdom of his mother. This wasn't just casual advice; it was described as an inspired utterance, suggesting her words carried divine weight. They weren't simply personal opinions but truths meant to guide his character, leadership, and decisions.

What's striking is that the entire Proverbs 31 passage begins not with a king's decree but with a woman's voice—a mother imparting wisdom to her son. In ancient cultures, a mother's role extended far beyond nurturing; she was a foundational teacher, instilling values that would shape future generations. Lemuel's mother didn't just instruct him on how to rule, she taught him how to live with integrity, justice, and compassion.

This verse challenges us to recognize the power of a woman's words, not just in motherhood but also in mentorship, leadership, and community. Women play a vital role in shaping the future through the wisdom they impart, the love they embody, and the truth they convey.

When we envision the Proverbs 31 woman, we often picture her as strong, dignified, and wise. But these qualities don't emerge in isolation; they are passed down, cultivated, and stewarded. The Proverbs 31 woman is more than a role model; she is the fruit of wise counsel and a legacy of truth.

Living in her image means honoring both the wisdom we receive and the wisdom we share. Whether you're a mother, sister, mentor, friend, or leader, your words matter. Just as his mother's voice shaped Lemuel, we too are called to receive wisdom and pass it on, nurturing others in love and truth.

IN HIS IMAGE

God, as our Father, is the ultimate source of wisdom. He lovingly instructs, shapes, and guides us, just as Lemuel's mother guided him. The wisdom she offered mirrors the way God teaches us—through Scripture, His Spirit, and the voices of those He places in our lives.

God's role as Father isn't distant or demanding; it's personal and compassionate. He corrects us not to shame us but to refine us. He leads not to control but to equip. His wisdom forms the foundation of a life lived with purpose and integrity.

Just as Lemuel's mother shaped her son to lead with justice and discernment, God shapes us so that we can carry His truth into the world. When we walk in His wisdom and share it with others, we reflect His love, justice, and light, leaving a legacy that points people back to Him.

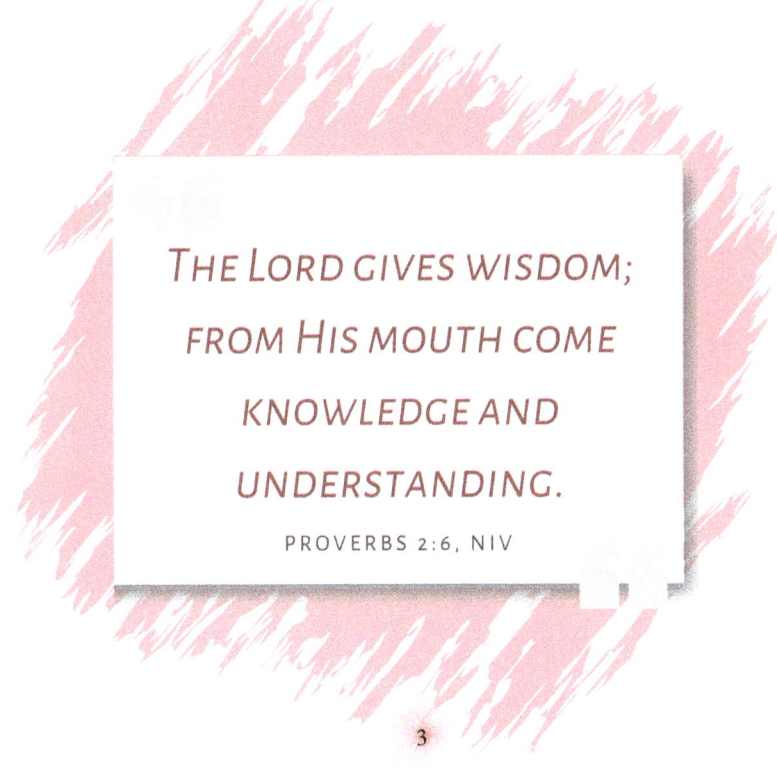

> *The Lord gives wisdom; from His mouth come knowledge and understanding.*
>
> PROVERBS 2:6, NIV

THINK ABOUT IT

Whose wisdom has helped shape the way you think, live, or lead?

_____
_____
_____
_____
_____
_____

Where in your life is God inviting you to speak His wisdom into someone else's journey?

_____
_____
_____
_____
_____
_____

LIVE THIS TODAY

My words carry wisdom when they're rooted in His heart.

Think of one person in your life who may benefit from God's wisdom or encouragement. Write down what you want to share with them—whether it is a truth from Scripture, a lesson you have learned, or a word of hope. Then plan when and how you will speak or send it. Let your words reflect God's heart.

_____

_____

_____

_____

_____

_____

_____

_____

_____

_____

_____

_____

_____

_____

NOTES

Focus

Do not spend your strength on women,
your vigor on those who ruin kings.

Proverbs 31:3

IN HER WALK

King Lemuel's mother issues a strong warning in this verse: be mindful of where you invest your energy. As a king, he had power, responsibility, and influence, but if his focus was misplaced—especially on relationships or distractions that drained his energy—his ability to lead effectively would suffer.

This wisdom applies to us just as much as it did to Lemuel. Where we place our focus determines the direction of our lives. We live in a world filled with distractions—social media, entertainment, unhealthy relationships, or even overcommitting to things that don't align with our values. These influences can slowly pull us away from our purpose if we're not intentional.

The Proverbs 31 woman is often praised for her diligence, strength, and wisdom, but she doesn't just happen upon these qualities. She is focused. She directs her time and energy toward things that matter, such as her faith, family, work, and calling. Her ability to be strong and effective comes from knowing what to invest in and what to avoid.

Losing focus doesn't happen overnight. It's often a slow drift—one compromise, one distraction, one misplaced priority at a time. Lemuel's mother warned him to stay alert. In the same way, we need to guard our focus against the subtle things that drain our energy, compromise our values, or pull us away from God's will.

This verse is also a call to examine our relationships. Are the people around us lifting us up, encouraging us in our faith, and keeping us accountable? Or are they pulling us away from what truly matters? The company we keep affects our focus, mindset, and spiritual growth.

By being intentional with our focus, we can live a life of integrity, purpose, and direction—one that honors God and reflects the wisdom of Proverbs 31.

IN HIS IMAGE

God, as our loving Father, leads us toward righteousness and truth so we don't get caught up in distractions that derail us. He provides wisdom to help us discern what is worthy of our time, energy, and attention.

Just as Lemuel's mother urged him to focus on his duties as a king, God calls us to live with intention. He cares about how we spend our lives, and He lovingly redirects us when we lose sight of what matters most. His correction is not punishment; it's guidance born of deep love.

To live in her image is to be mindful of where we direct our focus. When we guard our attention and invest in what truly matters, we align ourselves with God's will. As we choose to let go of what distracts us, we step fully into the identity and purpose He designed for us.

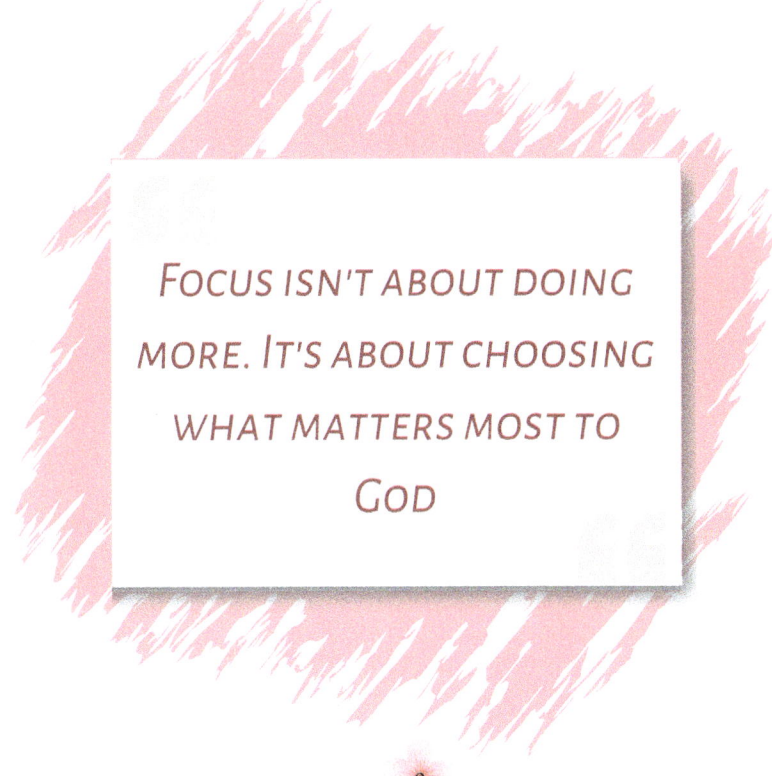

Focus isn't about doing more. It's about choosing what matters most to God

Think About It

What distractions are most likely to pull your focus away from the things that matter most?

___

___

___

___

___

___

___

Who or what helps you stay centered on your values and purpose?

___

___

___

___

___

___

___

LIVE THIS TODAY

Where I fix my focus shapes the life I live.

Write down three specific things that tend to distract you from your purpose. For each one, identify one practical step you can take this week to minimize or remove it. Ask God to help you stay focused on what truly matters.

_____

_____

_____

_____

_____

_____

_____

_____

_____

_____

_____

_____

_____

NOTES

Advocate

Use your voice and influence to advocate for justice and protect the vulnerable.

Proverbs 31:8

IN HER WALK

King Lemuel's mother didn't just teach him how to lead; she taught him the "why" of leadership. She urged him to advocate for those who could not defend themselves—the voiceless, the poor, and the oppressed. This verse highlights one of the most powerful aspects of leadership: the responsibility to stand for justice.

True leadership, whether in government, communities, workplaces, or personal relationships, is not about power for personal gain. It's about using influence to uplift others, especially those who are vulnerable. Lemuel's mother wanted him to lead with integrity, courage, and compassion. These qualities are just as relevant today as they were then.

In ancient times, the poor and marginalized had little to no rights. Their voices were ignored, and their needs were overlooked. Kings were expected to uphold justice, ensuring that those without power were seen and protected. The Proverbs 31 woman's wisdom wasn't just about running a household; it was about shaping a world that reflects God's justice and wholeness.

This wisdom extends beyond kings and rulers. We all have influence. Whether we realize it or not, our words, actions, and choices impact those around us. This verse challenges us to examine how we use our voice, influence, and resources. Are we speaking up when we see injustice? Are we advocating for those who are overlooked? Or are we remaining silent when our voice could bring change?

Speaking up isn't just about being loud. It's about being brave. It's choosing to stand in the gap for those who cannot stand for themselves. It's being a voice of hope in a world that often silences the weak.

IN HIS IMAGE

God is not only our loving Father, He is also our Judge—the One who sees every injustice and responds with truth and righteousness. As Judge, He defends the oppressed, lifts the brokenhearted, and brings justice to those who are wronged.

To reflect His image means we cannot stay silent when injustice surrounds us. Just as God stands for what is right, He invites us to do the same. Speaking up isn't about being perfect; it's about being aligned with His heart. When we choose to advocate for the voiceless, we partner with God's mission of restoration and wholeness.

Living in her image means living with courage. It means using our voice, influence, and resources to lift others up—not because it's easy, but because it's right. When we defend those who cannot defend themselves, we reflect the heart of a just and holy God.

WHEN WE SPEAK UP FOR OTHERS, WE REFLECT THE GOD WHO DEFENDS THE WEAK.

THINK ABOUT IT

Who in your life or your community might need you to speak up on their behalf?

_____

_____

_____

_____

_____

_____

What holds you back from using your voice when you see injustice?

_____

_____

_____

_____

_____

_____

LIVE THIS TODAY

Justice begins when I choose to speak up.

Write down one area in your life or community where you have seen injustice, silence, or neglect. Ask God how you can be an advocate in that space—whether through words, service, or simply standing with someone who feels unseen—and write down one step you can take this week.

_____

_____

_____

_____

_____

_____

_____

_____

_____

_____

_____

_____

_____

_____

NOTES

Just

Speak up and judge fairly; defend the rights of the poor and needy.

Proverbs 31:9

IN HER WALK

Lemuel's mother urges him to speak up, judge fairly, and defend the vulnerable. This isn't just a call to fairness; it's a call to restoration. Her counsel challenges her son to use his influence to bring justice that doesn't simply balance the scales but actively works to heal and uplift those who have been overlooked or oppressed.

True justice isn't just about making things "fair"; it's about making things whole. Lemuel's mother wanted him to understand that being a leader wasn't about power—it was about responsibility. His role wasn't to serve his own interests but to create a kingdom where dignity, righteousness, and compassion flourished.

Our world is filled with broken systems, fractured relationships, and deep physical, emotional, and spiritual wounds. We are called not just to be bystanders but to be agents of restoration. Whether it's through personal relationships, community service, or simply speaking truth in a way that uplifts others, we have a role in creating a world where justice and compassion work together.

Pursuing wholeness means looking beyond quick fixes or surface-level fairness. It calls us to lean into the hard work of healing, listening, and restoring. Justice isn't simply about punishing broken rules, but is founded on restoring shalom (wholeness and peace). God is the ultimate restorer of wholeness. His justice is not merely a system of rewards and consequences; it is rooted in love, redemption, and healing.

In His Image

When we think of God as Judge, we often imagine stern correction or punishment. However, Scripture paints a deeper picture, one in which God's justice is restorative, not just corrective. God defends the oppressed, lifts the brokenhearted, and restores what was lost. His judgment brings peace, order, and wholeness, not just verdicts. In one word, justice restores shalom.

To reflect His image means to pursue that kind of justice. We are invited to be restorers, not critics. Our role is not simply to point out what's wrong but to help bring healing where there's been harm.

Living in her image means embracing the work of restoration. It means choosing compassion over control, healing over revenge, and redemption over resignation. When we pursue wholeness in the lives of others, we echo the heart of the God who restores all things.

> God's justice doesn't just make things fair. It makes things whole.

THINK ABOUT IT

Where in your life or community do you see brokenness that needs healing?

_____

_____

_____

_____

_____

_____

How can you reflect God's justice by helping restore what's been lost or ignored?

_____

_____

_____

_____

_____

_____

_____

LIVE THIS TODAY
Justice restores what's been lost or broken.

Identify one person or situation in your life that feels fractured—whether emotionally, relationally, or socially. Write down one way you can actively take part in restoring wholeness this week, whether through encouragement, reconciliation, or practical help.

NOTES

NOBLE

A woman of noble character who can find? She is worth far more than rubies.

Proverbs 31:10

IN HER WALK

This verse introduces a woman whose true worth is found in the strength of her character, not in wealth, beauty, or status. The term "noble" refers to a person who consistently chooses what is good and just, even in difficult situations.

A noble character is built through daily decisions: choosing kindness over resentment, honesty over convenience, and faith over fear. These choices shape who we are and leave a lasting impact on our lives and those around us. To live in her image means cultivating a character rooted in love, integrity, service, and righteousness because these qualities reflect who God has called us to be.

In ancient Hebrew culture, noble character was often tied to one's faithfulness to covenant, whether with God, family, or community. The woman in this passage is described in terms typically reserved for warriors and leaders, highlighting her inner strength and unwavering commitment to righteousness. This wasn't common language for women at that time, making her example all the more striking. Her nobility wasn't inherited by status but cultivated through obedience, courage, and love in action.

She reminds us that true value comes from within, not from success or appearance. The noble woman is praised for her commitment to purpose and integrity, building her life on a foundation of faithfulness and wisdom.

This verse calls us to examine what we are building our lives upon: external success or the unshakable truth of God's wisdom. A woman of noble character is defined by who she is when no one is watching.

In His Image

God is the ultimate example of integrity. Everything He does is rooted in righteousness, love, and justice. His love is not conditional; it remains unchanged regardless of circumstances. He is faithful, steadfast, and true.

As women created in His image, we are called to reflect His love. The Proverbs 31 woman mirrors God's love by living a life that honors those around her. She doesn't act out of selfish ambition but chooses to serve, give, and love because her heart is aligned with God's.

To live in her image means allowing God's love to shape our character. As we grow in faith, our actions, decisions, and relationships should reflect His righteousness and kindness. The more we allow God to refine us, the more we become living examples of His love.

When we allow God's love to define us, our character begins to reflect His nature.
In His Image, Andrea John

THINK ABOUT IT

What daily choices are shaping your character? Are they rooted in God's truth or external pressure?

_____
_____
_____
_____
_____
_____

How can you reflect God's love and integrity more clearly in your relationships?

_____
_____
_____
_____
_____
_____

LIVE THIS TODAY

Noble character reflects God's heart, even in unseen moments.

Identify one area in your life where you want to grow in noble character. Write down one daily practice you can begin today that reflects God's integrity and love, even when no one is watching.

_____

_____

_____

_____

_____

_____

_____

_____

_____

_____

_____

_____

_____

_____

NOTES

Trustworthy

Her husband has full confidence in her and lacks nothing of value.

Proverbs 31:11

IN HER WALK

This verse paints a picture of a woman whose character and actions inspire complete confidence. Her husband fully trusts her because she has consistently proven herself to be reliable, honorable, and trustworthy. Their relationship is built on a foundation of trust, allowing them both to thrive.

Trust isn't something that happens overnight; it is earned through daily decisions and a pattern of dependability. The Proverbs 31 woman doesn't need to reassure her husband of her faithfulness constantly because her actions speak louder than words. She follows through on her commitments, acts with integrity, and creates an environment of security and stability for those she loves.

This principle extends beyond marriage. Trust is the foundation of every strong relationship—whether in friendships, within families, at work, or in our communities. Without trust, relationships become fragile, marked by doubt and uncertainty. But when trust is nurtured, it allows love, respect, and connection to grow.

In today's world, trust is often easily broken and difficult to rebuild. People struggle with past betrayals, dishonesty, and inconsistency. That's why it's so powerful when someone proves to be dependable, honest, and steadfast. The Proverbs 31 woman challenges us to be people who keep our word, act with integrity, and cultivate an atmosphere of trust wherever we go.

In the ancient Hebrew context, trust was inseparable from covenant faithfulness—the kind of relational loyalty God extended to His people. To be called trustworthy wasn't just about being nice or dependable; it meant someone could rest in the assurance of your word. The Proverbs 31 woman models this covenantal strength as she becomes a safe place. Her presence is steady, and her character gives others peace.

In His Image

God is the ultimate model of trustworthiness. Throughout Scripture, He is described as faithful, steadfast, and unchanging. He always keeps His promises, never fails in His love, and remains constant no matter the circumstances.

To live in her image is to reflect God's faithfulness in the way we interact with others. Just as God never fails in His commitment to us, we are called to be people who honor our word, follow through, and create a foundation of trust in our relationships.

Being trustworthy isn't just about keeping promises; it's about embodying God's reliability. In a world full of broken trust, we reflect His image when we remain steady, loyal, and true. When others experience our consistency, they glimpse the faithfulness of the One who never changes.

We reflect God's faithfulness when we choose to be steady, loyal, and true.

Think About It

What habits or patterns in your life help others see you as trustworthy?

_____
_____
_____
_____
_____
_____

Where is God calling you to rebuild trust or offer it to someone else?

_____
_____
_____
_____
_____
_____
_____

LIVE THIS TODAY

Trust grows when faithfulness becomes our way of life.

Think of a relationship where trust needs to be strengthened. Write down one practical step you can take today to build or rebuild that trust through honesty, follow-through, or grace.

_____

_____

_____

_____

_____

_____

_____

_____

_____

_____

_____

_____

_____

NOTES

Goodness

She brings him good, not harm, all the days of her life.

Proverbs 31:12

IN HER WALK

The Proverbs 31 woman is committed to bringing goodness into her relationships. The phrase "all the days of her life" suggests that goodness is not something she offers only when it's convenient, easy, or earned. Instead, she makes a conscious and daily choice to be a source of blessing, encouragement, and kindness.

Her actions are not reactionary; they are intentional. She doesn't allow circumstances, frustrations, or difficult people to dictate how she treats others. Instead, she creates an atmosphere of love, peace, and hope by consistently choosing to respond with kindness, patience, and grace.

This verse is a reminder that goodness is not passive; it is active. It is woven into our character through the choices we make each day. The Proverbs 31 woman doesn't just bring goodness when it's easy; she embodies goodness as a way of life. She understands that small, daily acts of kindness, such as a gentle word, a helping hand, or a moment of encouragement, can have a lasting impact.

Bringing good and not harm doesn't mean avoiding conflict or pretending everything is perfect. It means choosing love over bitterness, peace over division, and uplifting rather than tearing down.

In a world where negativity often spreads faster than kindness, we have the opportunity to be a source of light. We should not wait for the perfect moment to show goodness. Instead, we should intentionally create opportunities to uplift, encourage, and promote harmony in our relationships.

Goodness isn't just about what we do; it's about who we are becoming.

In His Image

God is the ultimate Creator, the perfect model of goodness. From the beginning, His goodness was revealed through the way He shaped the world with order, beauty, and love. After each act of creation, He called it "good," not because it was simply finished but because it reflected His intention to give life, bring joy, and establish peace.

When we choose to bring goodness into the world, we echo the heart of our Creator. Just as God intentionally formed an environment where life could flourish, we are called to create spaces of trust, love, and grace. Goodness is about building a consistent legacy of love and faithfulness.

To live in her image means to create with care, speak with intention, and act with compassion. When we reflect God's creative goodness, our relationships and communities become places where His love is known and experienced.

The Lord is good to all; He has compassion on all He has made.
Psalm 145:9, NIV

THINK ABOUT IT

What small choices can you make today to bring goodness into someone's life?

_____
_____
_____
_____
_____
_____
_____

Are there patterns in your relationships that need more kindness, consistency, or care?

_____
_____
_____
_____
_____
_____
_____

LIVE THIS TODAY

Goodness flows from who I am becoming.

Think of one person who could use a reminder that they matter. Write down a specific way you will show them today—through a kind word, helpful action, or quiet encouragement—that they are valued.

_____

_____

_____

_____

_____

_____

_____

_____

_____

_____

_____

_____

_____

_____

NOTES

WHOLEHEARTED

She selects wool and flax and works with eager hands. She is like the merchant ships, bringing her food from afar. She gets up while it is still night; she provides food for her family and portions for her female servants.

Proverbs 31:13-15

IN HER WALK

The Proverbs 31 woman lives with wholehearted devotion. She doesn't just complete tasks; she puts her heart into everything she does. Whether choosing materials for her household or preparing food in the early morning, her work is fueled by intention, care, and love.

Her effort is not hurried or half-hearted. She selects wool and flax, materials valued for their strength and beauty. This reflects her desire to bring not just the necessary but the best into her home. Her hands are eager, not reluctant, showing that she views her work as meaningful and her service as sacred.

She's described as being like merchant ships, meaning this woman is reliable, far-reaching, and full of provision. She rises early to care for her household, not because she has to, but because she chooses to. Her love is evident in her actions, creating an atmosphere of peace, order, and honor in her home.

This passage isn't just about chores or responsibilities. It's about the spirit in which we live and serve. In a world that often celebrates busyness, the Proverbs 31 woman shows us the value of doing things with purpose. She reminds us that when we work with a wholehearted spirit, even the smallest tasks carry significance.

In ancient cultures, early rising and bringing goods from afar were signs of strength, leadership, and devotion to others. This woman embodies those qualities not by dominating but by serving with excellence and presence. Her energy is not driven by pressure; it flows from a heart anchored in love.

In His Image

God, as Creator, embodies wholeheartedness. Everything He does is intentional, beautiful, and life-giving. He didn't create the world in a rush or out of obligation; He shaped every detail with love and purpose. When He saw what He had made, He called it good.

We reflect His image when we bring that same wholehearted devotion into our lives. Whether we're serving our families, engaging in our work, or building relationships, our effort can become a form of worship when it is offered with sincerity and love.

To live in her image is to live with heart. It's about choosing to approach each day not just with duty but with delight, letting our hands, words, and time be shaped by the intentional love of the One who formed us.

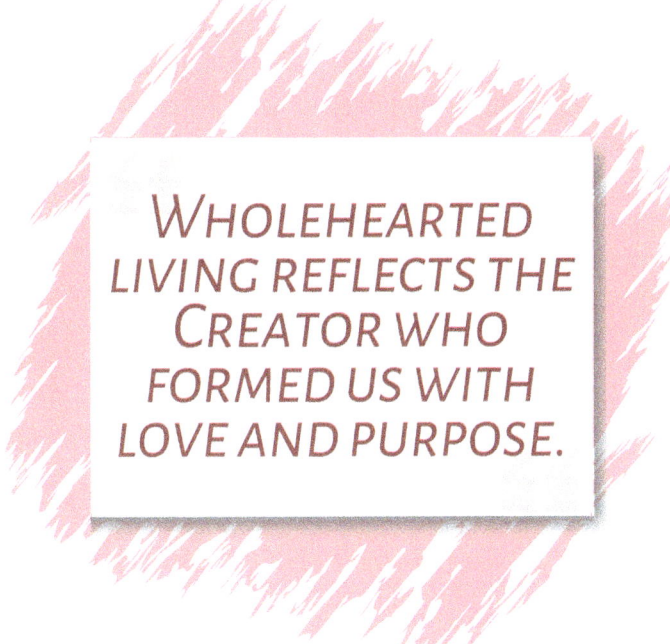

WHOLEHEARTED LIVING REFLECTS THE CREATOR WHO FORMED US WITH LOVE AND PURPOSE.

Think About It

Do you approach your daily work with a spirit of obligation or devotion?

_____
_____
_____
_____
_____
_____

How can you bring more love and intention into the small things you do today?

_____
_____
_____
_____
_____
_____

LIVE THIS TODAY

Wholeheartedness turns ordinary moments into sacred offerings.

Choose one task or responsibility you often rush through. Write down how you will do it today with greater love, presence, or intention. Afterward, notice and record how that shift impacts your attitude.

_____
_____
_____
_____
_____
_____
_____
_____
_____
_____
_____
_____
_____
_____
_____

NOTES

Diligent

She selects wool and flax and works with eager hands.

Proverbs 31:13

IN HER WALK

The woman in this verse is a model of intentionality, diligence, and joy in her work. She does not approach her responsibilities with reluctance or mere obligation; she embraces them with eager hands. This phrase speaks to her willingness, energy, and commitment to excellence in all she does.

Her work is not rushed or careless but thoughtful and purposeful. She carefully selects materials like wool and flax, knowing that the quality of what she chooses will impact what she produces. This reveals a heart that values excellence over convenience, craftsmanship over shortcuts, and purpose over mere productivity.

In today's fast-paced world, we often rush through tasks, multitask endlessly, or see work as a burden rather than an opportunity. But this verse challenges us to reframe our perspective. Instead of treating daily responsibilities as a checklist to complete, what if we approached them as acts of love?

The Proverbs 31 woman reminds us that even the most ordinary tasks can be sacred when done with purpose. Whether at work, at home, or in our communities, our diligence can be a reflection of our values, a testimony to our character, and a way to bless those around us.

Diligence is more than hard work; it is love in action.

IN HIS IMAGE

When God created the world, He crafted each detail with care, purpose, and excellence. He took His time, and when He finished, He declared it "good."

God's work wasn't just functional; it was beautiful. His diligence brought order to chaos, filled empty spaces with life, and established rhythms of light and rest. He created a world designed to flourish.

To live in her image means to adopt this same spirit of diligence. Whether in our work, relationships, or personal growth, we are called to approach life with intentionality and attention to detail. Our diligence reflects God's nature and shows that we value what He has entrusted to us.

By bringing intention and commitment into our daily lives, we mirror God's heart as Creator. We honor Him not only by what we do but by how we do it—with focus, excellence, and love.

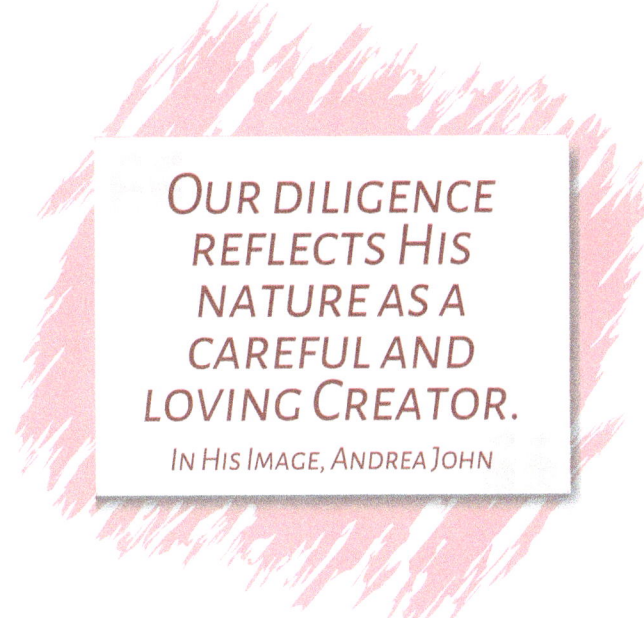

> OUR DILIGENCE REFLECTS HIS NATURE AS A CAREFUL AND LOVING CREATOR.
> *In His Image, Andrea John*

THINK ABOUT IT

What would change if you saw your daily work as sacred rather than stressful?

_____
_____
_____
_____
_____
_____

Where can you show more care, focus, or joy in how you approach your responsibilities?

_____
_____
_____
_____
_____
_____
_____

LIVE THIS TODAY

My diligence reflects the careful heart of my Creator.

Choose one task you usually rush through. Describe how you will approach it today with renewed purpose, patience, and joy. As you complete it, offer it to God as an act of worship.

NOTES

Excellence

She is like the merchant ships, bringing her food from afar.

Proverbs 31:14

IN HER WALK

This verse beautifully illustrates the Proverbs 31 woman's commitment to excellence. She is compared to merchant ships, which in ancient times traveled long distances to acquire goods from far-off lands. These ships symbolized abundance, quality, and reliability. They didn't settle for what was immediately available; they brought home the best, enriching their communities with value and variety.

For the original audience, comparing a woman to merchant ships would have been both poetic and powerful. It highlighted her as someone dependable, far-reaching in her efforts, and willing to go beyond what was expected.

The Proverbs 31 woman goes the extra mile, not just in grand gestures but in small, consistent choices that reflect her devotion to nurturing a life of meaning. Her excellence isn't about being flawless; it's about purpose-driven effort, choosing quality over ease, faithfulness over shortcuts, and commitment over complacency.

This verse challenges us to reflect on how we approach our own work and responsibilities. Excellence is not about seeking applause; it's about serving others well and honoring God with our effort.

The metaphor of the merchant ship also reminds us that the journey matters. Excellence isn't just about the result; it's about the intentional choices we make along the way. Taking the extra step may require more effort, but it is always worthwhile.

Excellence is about giving our best, even in the unseen moments. It is about showing up with dedication, even when it is inconvenient. It is about elevating our work, knowing that everything we do can be an offering to God.

In His Image

God is the ultimate model of excellence. From the vast galaxies to the smallest seed, His creation reflects care, detail, and intentional design. Nothing He does is rushed or careless. When He formed the world, He stepped back and declared it good, not because it was merely complete but because it was beautiful, ordered, and filled with purpose.

As Creator, God's excellence reveals His heart. He gives His best in all He makes, and we are invited to reflect that same spirit in our lives.

To live in her image means to bring that Creator-like excellence into everything we do. Whether preparing a meal, leading a team, writing a note of encouragement, or quietly showing up for someone in need, our diligence and care become reflections of His glory.

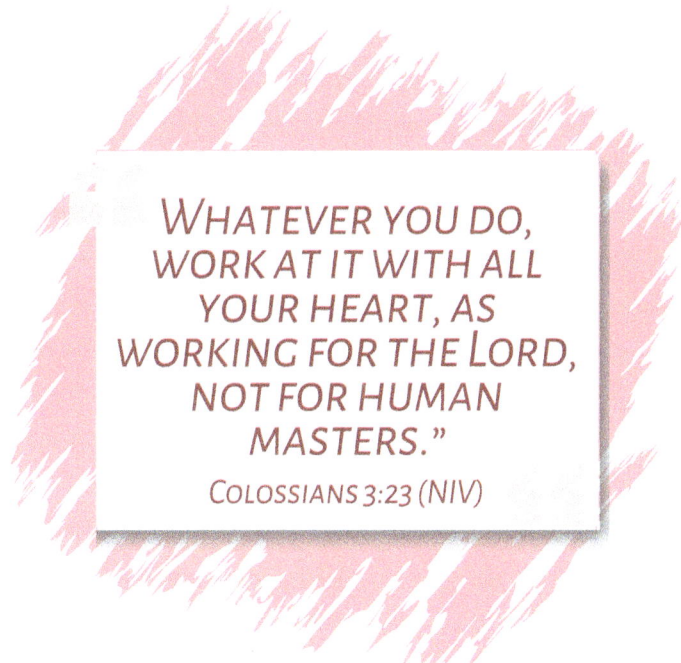

Whatever you do, work at it with all your heart, as working for the Lord, not for human masters."
Colossians 3:23 (NIV)

THINK ABOUT IT

Where in your life have you been tempted to settle for "good enough" instead of giving your best?

_____
_____
_____
_____
_____
_____

What's one way you can elevate the quality of your work or service this week?

_____
_____
_____
_____
_____
_____

LIVE THIS TODAY

Excellence honors God and brings lasting value to others.

Choose one task, responsibility, or relationship where you usually take shortcuts or disengage. Write down how you'll approach it differently today—with care, intention, and a heart of worship. Then, put your plan into action.

NOTES

RESPONSIBLE

She gets up while it is still night; she provides food for her family and portions for her female servants.

Proverbs 31:15

IN HER WALK

Responsibility is a character trait of the Proverbs 31 woman. She wakes before dawn, not because she has to but because she is committed to ensuring the well-being of those in her care. Her actions reflect intentionality, planning, and a heart that prioritizes others.

Historically, preparing food required great effort, foresight, and time. She doesn't wait until her household wakes up to figure out what they need; she anticipates and prepares in advance. This level of responsibility extends beyond providing, as it becomes an act of love.

Her early rising is symbolic of a proactive mindset. She doesn't just respond to the day as it comes; she prepares for it. She ensures that her household has what they need before they even realize they need it. True responsibility isn't only about reacting to the present; it is about thoughtfully planning for the future.

In today's world, this verse invites us to examine our own approach to responsibility. Are we intentional in our planning? Do we prepare thoughtfully for our families, our work, and our commitments? Or do we find ourselves constantly scrambling to keep up?

Responsibility is more than managing tasks; it is about creating an atmosphere of peace, stability, and support for those we serve. When we prepare ahead of time, we reduce stress, eliminate chaos, and allow ourselves to be fully present in the moment.

In His Image

God, as our Father, demonstrates perfect responsibility. From the beginning, He prepared the earth for humanity with care and intention. Before Adam and Eve were formed, every detail was in place.

Throughout Scripture, we see His foresight: manna in the wilderness, prophetic voices before crisis, Jesus sent before we even knew we needed Him. God doesn't scramble to react; He prepares in love.

To live in her image is to reflect that same heart. We plan, prepare, and provide not out of pressure, but out of love. Our forethought mirrors God's faithfulness and creates safety for those we care for.

True responsibility begins with love and leads to peace.

Think About It

What area of your life would benefit from more intentional planning?

_____
_____
_____
_____
_____
_____
_____

How can you show care through preparation this week?

_____
_____
_____
_____
_____
_____
_____

LIVE THIS TODAY

Responsibility done in love creates peace and stability for others.

Identify one task that often causes you stress. Write down a simple plan today for how you'll approach it with greater peace and preparation. Then, carry it out as an intentional act of love.

NOTES

Visionary

She considers a field and buys it; out of her earnings she plants a vineyard.

Proverbs 31:16

IN HER WALK

The Proverbs 31 woman is discerning and strategic. This verse gives us a glimpse into her financial and practical wisdom. She doesn't act impulsively; she considers the field. She evaluates its potential and makes a thoughtful investment. Her decision is not about ownership for its own sake but for growth, sustainability, and provision.

Once she buys the field, she doesn't stop there. She plants a vineyard, showing vision for the future. Vineyards take time and care before yielding fruit. Her actions reveal patience, planning, and a commitment to lasting impact.

This kind of stewardship speaks to more than land or money. It reflects how we manage everything God entrusts to us, such as our time, energy, finances, gifts, and relationships. Are we making decisions that reflect our values and honor God's purpose?

In a world driven by instant results, this verse reminds us to be prayerful and purposeful. Vision requires faith. Wise investment involves both foresight and trust, believing that God will bring fruit at the right time.

In the ancient world, a vineyard was a long-term investment. The Proverbs 31 woman models what it means to live with vision: to see potential where others see inconvenience and to sow seeds today that will bless future generations.

IN HIS IMAGE

God, as Creator, is the perfect visionary. From the beginning, He shaped the world with intention, preparing it to support and sustain life. Nothing was created without purpose or foresight.

Throughout Scripture, God provides not just for the moment but for the future. He sends provision before need arises, speaks promises generations in advance, and works through seasons we do not yet see. His vision is eternal and yet deeply personal.

To live in her image means to reflect that creative, forward-looking nature. We don't live only for today; we sow with purpose, build with wisdom, and trust that God will bring growth in His time.

> LET US NOT BECOME WEARY IN DOING GOOD, FOR AT THE PROPER TIME WE WILL REAP A HARVEST IF WE DO NOT GIVE UP.
>
> GALATIANS 6:9, NIV

THINK ABOUT IT

What area of your life could benefit from greater long-term vision?

_____
_____
_____
_____
_____
_____

Are your current decisions building toward something that reflects God's purpose?

_____
_____
_____
_____
_____
_____

LIVE THIS TODAY

Vision is faith in action; investing now in what will bless later.

Write down one area where God is asking you to invest with faith—trusting Him with the outcome. It could be a relationship, a habit, or a dream. Then, identify one step you can take today to plant the seed and move forward.

_____

_____

_____

_____

_____

_____

_____

_____

_____

_____

_____

_____

NOTES

Resilient

She sets about her work vigorously; her arms are strong for her tasks.

Proverbs 31:17

IN HER WALK

This verse paints a vivid picture of a woman who doesn't hesitate or hold back but moves with purpose. The Proverbs 31 woman works vigorously, a word that implies intensity, energy, and wholeheartedness. She doesn't approach her responsibilities with dread or duty but with strength and a steady spirit.

The phrase "her arms are strong for her tasks" speaks not only to physical strength but also to inner resilience—the kind of strength formed through consistent faithfulness and trust in God. Her strength is rooted in character, built by showing up daily with resolve, even when it's hard.

What is resilience? It is the ability to recover from difficulty, adapt through change, and persevere with hope. It is not about suppressing emotion or avoiding hardship but about returning to our source of strength again and again. Resilience is a heart anchored in truth, able to bend without breaking and brave enough to try again after a setback.

Today, our assignments may look different—parenting, leading, serving, or healing—but the call remains: press forward with a heart anchored in God's strength. Resilience is not about pushing through exhaustion or pretending everything is okay. It is returning to God when times get tough and drawing from His presence when yours feels empty. It is rising when it would be easier to retreat, choosing to continue when you could quit, and believing even when circumstances say otherwise.

The Proverbs 31 woman reminds us that resilience is not loud or flashy; it is faithful. That kind of faithfulness, built over time, becomes a testimony of grace, grit, and unwavering trust in the One who strengthens us for every task.

In His Image

God, as Light, is constant, even when circumstances shift. His light doesn't flicker in the dark or retreat in the storm. It remains steady and unwavering, guiding us forward.

To live in her image is to reflect that same resilience. Just as God's light brings clarity and hope, our perseverance through trials can shine a light for others. Resilience isn't about having all the answers but about standing firm in faith when everything else feels unsteady.

When we draw strength from God's unchanging presence, our endurance becomes more than survival—it becomes a testimony. We don't shine because we are unshakable but because He is.

Resilience is strength rooted in faith.

THINK ABOUT IT

Where in your life are you being called to show up with resilient strength?

_____

_____

_____

_____

_____

_____

How does your perseverance reflect the light of God to others?

_____

_____

_____

_____

_____

_____

LIVE THIS TODAY

Resilience is faithfulness in motion.

Write down one area where you've felt weary or discouraged. Ask God for strength, then choose one small step—no matter how simple—you'll take today to keep showing up with faith and purpose.

NOTES

Purposeful

She sees that her trading is profitable,
and her lamp does not go out at night.

Proverbs 31:18

IN HER WALK

This verse highlights the Proverbs 31 woman's ability to recognize the value of her work. Her trading is profitable not just in financial return but in purpose and impact. She is discerning and intentional in how she invests her time, energy, and effort. She understands that what she does matters, and that understanding shapes how she lives.

The phrase "her lamp does not go out at night" speaks volumes. In ancient times, lamps were a symbol of presence, safety, and care. She isn't burning herself out; she is staying grounded in her purpose, knowing her light impacts those around her.

This verse invites us to look at our own work not through the lens of performance or productivity but through purpose. In a world that ties worth to outcomes, God invites us to see value in faithfulness. The invisible, daily work of love, service, and surrender matters deeply to Him.

The Proverbs 31 woman reminds us that purpose fuels sustainability. When we understand the "why" behind what we do, we work with more joy and less striving. We shift from seeking approval to walking in alignment. Our tasks become offerings, and our responsibilities become sacred.

When we live with purpose, we shine. That light endures because it is fueled by something deeper than recognition. It is rooted in knowing our work matters to God.

IN HIS IMAGE

God, as Creator, designed the world with intention. Every detail, from the stars in the sky to the breath in our lungs, was crafted with meaning. Nothing He formed is random or without purpose. Creation itself testifies to His vision.

When God made humanity in His image, He placed that same design for purpose within us. We were created to flourish, contribute, and reflect His creativity through the work of our hands.

To live in her image is to see our daily tasks as expressions of God's purposeful design flowing through us.

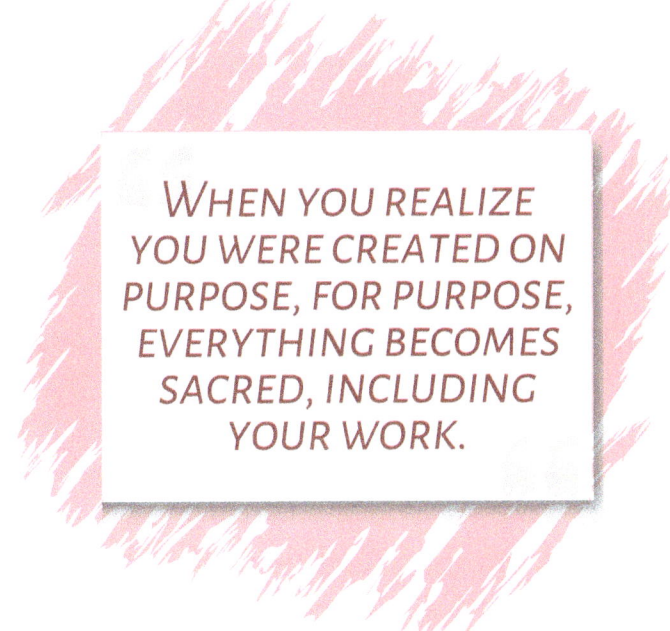

WHEN YOU REALIZE YOU WERE CREATED ON PURPOSE, FOR PURPOSE, EVERYTHING BECOMES SACRED, INCLUDING YOUR WORK.

THINK ABOUT IT

What daily task have you undervalued that actually carries deep purpose?

_____
_____
_____
_____
_____
_____

How would your work change if you saw it as sacred instead of routine?

_____
_____
_____
_____
_____
_____
_____

LIVE THIS TODAY

Purpose turns the ordinary into something sacred.

Think of one thing you truly enjoy doing, something that fills you with energy and joy. Write about why it gives you a sense of purpose. Then, consider how you can offer it to God and intentionally use it to bless others today.

NOTES

Skillfull

In her hand she holds the distaff and grasps the spindle with her fingers.

Proverbs 31:19

IN HER WALK

Proverbs 31:19 gives us a quiet yet powerful picture of the Proverbs 31 woman at work. With distaff and spindle in hand, she engages in the intricate and necessary task of spinning thread, an act that required great skill, patience, and focus in her day. This wasn't glamorous work, but it was meaningful. She did it with care, dignity, and intention.

While the tools may be outdated, the principle is timeless. The distaff and spindle represent whatever tools we hold today, such as laptops, aprons, pens, brooms, spreadsheets, or pans. It is not the tool that defines the value; it is the heart and skill behind it.

In a culture that often celebrates speed and productivity, we can forget the beauty of doing things well. This verse reminds us that how we work matters. Skillfulness is about commitment to growth, thoughtful action, and love poured into every detail.

When we view our work as sacred, even repetitive or unnoticed tasks take on meaning. The Proverbs 31 woman teaches us that excellence doesn't require a spotlight. Her hands move with intention because her heart knows the value of what she is building.

We honor God when we work with care. Every stitch, sweep, click, or word can become an offering. Our skill becomes an extension of our worship, and our labor becomes a legacy.

In His Image

God, as Creator, is the master craftsman. Every detail of creation, from the orbits of stars to the veins in leaves, reflects skill, beauty, and purpose. He didn't rush or overlook; He called His work "very good."

When we work with care and excellence, we reflect that same creative heart. We don't need to be famous or flawless, only faithful. Every task done with intention becomes sacred. God sees the process, not just the product. He values the quiet, careful work we do with love.

To live in her image is to embrace the artistry of ordinary moments. Our work, when done skillfully and for God, becomes more than effort. It becomes worship.

SKILLFUL WORK DONE IN LOVE REFLECTS THE INTENTIONAL HEART OF OUR CREATOR.

THINK ABOUT IT

What tool do you use most in your work or daily life? How does it reflect your heart?

___

How might God be inviting you to bring more intentionality to the way you work?

___

LIVE THIS TODAY
Skill grows where intention meets love.

Identify one skill you feel called to develop, something that will help you serve others or steward your responsibilities with greater excellence. Write it down. Then, list two immediate and practical steps you can take this week to grow in that skill.

NOTES

Generous

She opens her arms to the poor and extends her hands to the needy.

Proverbs 31:20

IN HER WALK

This verse beautifully portrays the Proverbs 31 woman as someone who lives with open arms and hands. Her generosity flows from a heart that is sensitive to the needs of others, not only within her home but also in her broader community. She doesn't wait to be asked; she reaches out willingly and freely, offering what she has to those who need it most.

What stands out is that her generosity isn't rooted in abundance but in awareness and compassion. She gives because she sees the need and cares deeply. Whether she offers food, support, time, or comfort, her willingness reflects a life centered on love. It is not about how much she has but the heart with which she gives it.

Generosity isn't limited to finances. It includes presence, empathy, and encouragement. Even a listening ear or a kind word can be a gift of profound value. In our fast-paced lives, it's easy to overlook these moments, but this verse invites us to slow down, notice, care, and act.

The Proverbs 31 woman teaches us that generosity is not just an occasional act; it is a way of life. Her compassion compels her to move, and her willingness to give leaves a lasting impact.

When we give from where we are, with what we have, in love, we live purposefully and powerfully. Generosity is measured by the heart behind the gift, not the size of it.

IN HIS IMAGE

God is Love. His generosity is the purest expression of that love. From creation to the cross, God gives with abundance, not because we have earned it but because it is His nature to do so. John 3:16 says it best: "For God so loved the world that He gave..." His giving is unconditional, sacrificial, and constant.

To live in her image is to reflect this divine love in action. When we open our hands to others, we mirror the heart of a God who never withholds His goodness. Love always gives, and it overflows into generosity.

Our calling isn't just to love with words but to express that love through tangible acts of care, compassion, and presence. Whether big or small, our gifts carry God's heart when they are given in love.

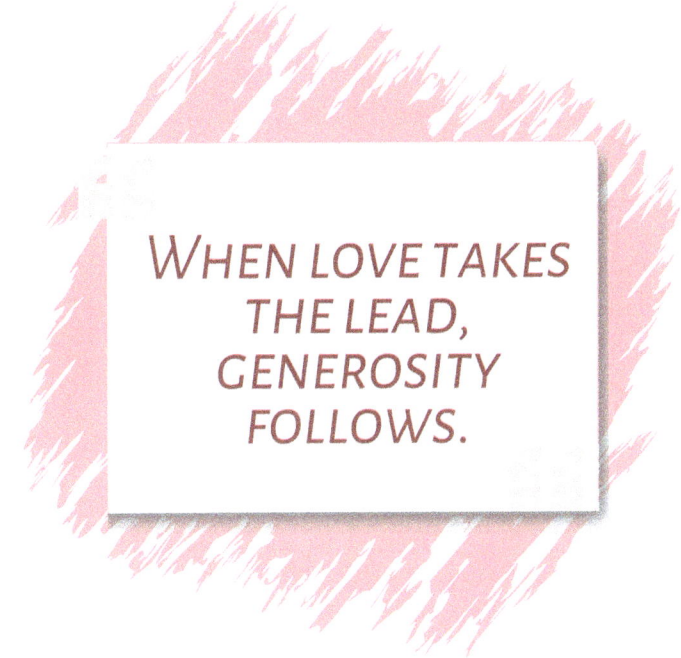

WHEN LOVE TAKES THE LEAD, GENEROSITY FOLLOWS.

THINK ABOUT IT

When was the last time someone's small act of generosity impacted you?

_____
_____
_____
_____
_____

What holds you back from giving more freely? Time, energy, or presence?

_____
_____
_____
_____
_____
_____
_____

LIVE THIS TODAY
Generosity begins where love overflows.

List one way you can give today—not with money, but with presence. Choose someone to encourage, support, or simply show up for, and write down how you will give in love.

_____
_____
_____
_____
_____
_____
_____
_____
_____
_____
_____
_____
_____

NOTES

KIND

She opens her arms to the poor and extends her hands to the needy.

Proverbs 31:20

IN HER WALK

This verse portrays the Proverbs 31 woman as someone who not only notices the needs around her but also actively responds. With open arms and extended hands, she embodies a lifestyle of kindness and compassion.

Her kindness is intentional, not reactive. She doesn't wait for people to come to her; instead, she moves toward them. She is attuned to others' suffering and offers help freely, not out of obligation but from genuine empathy. She understands that kindness is more than a feeling; it is love in action.

In ancient culture, generosity toward the poor and vulnerable was seen as an expression of true righteousness. The Proverbs 31 woman lives this out with humility and grace. Her example reminds us that kindness isn't just for our inner circle but for anyone in need of hope or support.

In today's fast-paced, self-focused world, it's easy to grow numb to the needs around us. Yet this verse calls us to be present, to truly see others, and to respond. Kindness doesn't need to be loud. It can be a quiet word, a simple favor, or a gentle act of compassion. When expressed in love, it carries lasting power.

The Proverbs 31 woman teaches us that kindness isn't weakness; it is strength guided by grace. It is the kind of love that heals.

In His Image

God, as Love, is the source of all true kindness. His love is generous, compassionate, and endlessly patient. He sees us in our need and responds with mercy. His kindness lifts, restores, and never runs out.

God's kindness is not based on what we deserve but on who He is. He gives, forgives, and welcomes us time and time again. His love moves toward us, not away, even in our weakness.

To live in her image is to reflect that kind of love in action. When we choose to be kind, we reflect the heart of a God who never withholds compassion. We become vessels of healing in a world desperate for gentleness.

KINDNESS IS THE ECHO OF GOD'S LOVE IN ACTION.

THINK ABOUT IT

When has someone's kindness changed your perspective or lifted your spirit?

_____
_____
_____
_____
_____
_____

Where might God be asking you to move toward someone today, even in a small way?

_____
_____
_____
_____
_____
_____

LIVE THIS TODAY
Kindness is love made visible.

Think of one small act of kindness you can offer someone outside your usual circle. Write it down, then carry it out without seeking recognition or expecting anything in return.

_____
_____
_____
_____
_____
_____
_____
_____
_____
_____
_____
_____
_____

NOTES

PROACTIVE

When it snows, she has no fear for her household; for all of them are clothed in scarlet.

Proverbs 31:21

IN HER WALK

This verse reveals the Proverbs 31 woman as proactive. She lives with wisdom, readiness, and love. When winter comes, she is not afraid. Her household is already clothed in scarlet, wrapped in warmth because she made the choice to prepare ahead of time.

"Scarlet" represents both beauty and insulation. Her care doesn't just meet basic needs; it also brings comfort. Her preparation isn't motivated by anxiety or perfectionism but by love. She doesn't wait for a crisis to act; she moves before it is needed, creating peace through her foresight.

Being proactive is more than planning meals or stocking up on coats. It is about the heart behind the planning. It is about seeing ahead, caring enough to anticipate the needs of those we love, and responding with quiet strength.

In today's world, being proactive can mean providing emotional support, budgeting wisely, or establishing routines that bring stability to our homes. It might mean praying over future decisions, having hard conversations early, or teaching our children truths they will need later.

The Proverbs 31 woman reminds us that we don't wait for storms to find shelter. We act now, in the light, so we are not overcome in the dark.

To be proactive is to love with foresight. It is to be anchored in the present while faithfully looking ahead, choosing steady, thoughtful care over reactive panic.

In His Image

God, as Father, models the perfect example of loving foresight. He never scrambles to meet our needs; He sees them before we do. From preparing Eden for Adam to sending Jesus for our salvation, God consistently moves in advance, covering us with His love and provision.

His plans are never rushed, and His timing is never off. He prepares not out of fear but out of wisdom and care.

To live in her image is to mirror the Father's heart. We anticipate the needs of those we love and create environments where peace and provision go hand in hand. Our proactive care reflects His steady, nurturing presence.

Being proactive reveals our trust in God to show up faithfully today so others can rest in the safety of tomorrow.

Peace grows where love prepares in advance.

THINK ABOUT IT

What's one area in your life where God has already gone ahead of you?

_____
_____
_____
_____
_____
_____
_____

How can you begin preparing now for a need that may come later?

_____
_____
_____
_____
_____
_____
_____

LIVE THIS TODAY

To be proactive is to prepare in love.

Choose one small area where you can prepare for a future need—spiritual, emotional, or practical. Write it down, then take the first proactive step to create peace in your home or relationships.

NOTES

Caring

She makes coverings for her bed; she is clothed in fine linen and purple.

Proverbs 31:22

IN HER WALK

This verse beautifully illustrates the Proverbs 31 woman's ability to care deeply, not only for others but also for herself. She "makes coverings for her bed," creating an environment of rest, beauty, and comfort. Her care begins at home, in the sacred space where bodies are restored and hearts find peace. Her home is tended with purpose, and so is her heart. She clothes herself "in fine linen and purple," a sign of dignity and intentionality.

In biblical times, purple was the color of royalty, and fine linen symbolized high quality and refinement. Her clothing wasn't about vanity; it was a declaration of value. She understood that caring for herself was not selfish but necessary.

Too often, modern women are praised for their exhaustion and self-neglect. Yet this woman reminds us that rest, beauty, and self-care are not indulgences; they are acts of stewardship. You cannot pour from an empty vessel. She ensures her cup is full so that when she serves, it comes from abundance rather than depletion.

This verse calls us to redefine what it means to care. Caring is not just cleaning, cooking, or helping others; it is also tending to the soul. It is waking up and deciding that your well-being matters too. It is understanding that God made you worthy of dignity, and your life is worth honoring.

Whether it is preparing a restful space, choosing clothes that bring confidence, or carving out time to recharge, these small acts can be holy. When we care for ourselves with intention, we echo the heart of the Father who loves us without condition and invite others to do the same.

In His Image

God, as Love, is deeply invested in our care and renewal. After six days of creating a world filled with beauty, order, and life, He rested—not from exhaustion but to model rhythm and restoration. The seventh day, the Sabbath, was the first thing God declared holy. He considered it so important that He later included it among the Ten Commandments, not as a restriction but as a gift.

Sabbath means to pause, cease striving, and create space for communion with God, restoration of the soul, and enjoyment of our labor. God cares not only that we give and serve but also that we rest and receive.

To live in her image is to embrace this sacred rhythm. Just as God wove rest into the fabric of creation, we are called to honor rest as an act of love.

REST IS SACRED—
IT'S WORSHIP.

THINK ABOUT IT

What area of your life is in need of intentional care right now?

_____
_____
_____
_____
_____
_____

How might your self-care become an act of worship this week?

_____
_____
_____
_____
_____
_____

LIVE THIS TODAY

When I care for myself, I honor the God who calls me worthy.

Write down one specific way you can tend to your own needs this week—emotionally, physically, or spiritually. Then list one step you'll take to make it happen.

NOTES

Integrity

Her husband is respected at the city gate, where he takes his seat among the elders of the land.

Proverbs 31:23

IN HER WALK

This verse reveals a profound truth: integrity not only shapes our personal lives but also influences the people closest to us. The Proverbs 31 woman is so consistent in character and honorable in her actions that her husband is respected among the city's leaders. He sits at the city gate—a place of public decision-making—not merely because of his own merit but also because of the woman who stands beside him.

Her life radiates wisdom, trustworthiness, and strength. This kind of character does not develop overnight; it is formed in the unseen moments of faithfulness, humility, and doing what is right when no one is watching. Her choices create an atmosphere of honor that extends beyond her household and into the community. Her husband is respected not only for who he is but also because of the honor she brings to their shared name.

In ancient Israel, the city gate was a symbolic place where elders and leaders gathered to make decisions, resolve disputes, and uphold justice. To be seated at the gate was a mark of esteem. This verse honors the woman behind the man, acknowledging the strength, loyalty, and integrity she brought into their relationship and into public view.

Integrity in our world today may sometimes feel undervalued, but it remains a cornerstone of character. When we consistently show up with honesty, compassion, and purpose, we leave a legacy that strengthens those we love. Our families, friendships, and communities are shaped by the quiet obedience we demonstrate. The Proverbs 31 woman reminds us that powerful influence is often built in small, faithful moments, and that integrity lived out daily creates a foundation of respect that lifts others higher.

In His Image

God, as Judge, is the ultimate example of integrity. He is just, trustworthy, and unwavering in His character. His judgments are not influenced by appearances or human opinion; they are rooted in truth.

To live in her image is to reflect God's unwavering commitment to what is right. Our integrity becomes a mirror of His holiness, a steady light that brings clarity and confidence to those around us. When we choose truth, even when it is difficult, we align ourselves with the nature of the One who sees and knows all.

God's integrity is not cold or detached; it is deeply relational. He invites us to live in a way that strengthens trust, nurtures honor, and builds a legacy of truthfulness. Integrity is revealed when our actions consistently reflect the truth of God's character.

THINK ABOUT IT

What does living with integrity look like in your daily life right now?

_____
_____
_____
_____
_____
_____

Is there a hidden area where God may be calling you to bring more truth and alignment?

_____
_____
_____
_____
_____
_____

LIVE THIS TODAY

Integrity strengthens everyone it touches.

Write down one situation where you're tempted to compromise your values—at work, in a relationship, or in a daily decision. Describe what it would look like to respond with integrity instead. Then, take one intentional step today to align your actions with that truth.

_____

_____

_____

_____

_____

_____

_____

_____

_____

_____

_____

_____

_____

_____

NOTES

Driven

She makes linen garments and sells them, and supplies the merchants with sashes.

Proverbs 31:24

IN HER WALK

The Proverbs 31 woman doesn't wait for purpose to find her because she lives on purpose. This verse paints her as resourceful, entrepreneurial, and highly intentional in her work. She not only creates high-quality garments from valuable materials like linen but also brings them to the marketplace, serving her community and contributing economically to her household.

Her drive is fueled by purpose, not pressure. She doesn't hustle for approval; she offers her work as an extension of her calling. Creating and selling garments in ancient times wasn't a simple or glamorous task. It required time, precision, and patience—qualities she carried with grace. Linen was prized for its durability and beauty, and the sashes she provided reflected her attention to both function and style.

This woman is driven not by perfectionism but by commitment. She understands that work done with love and excellence becomes a blessing to herself, her family, and her community. She is not only diligent in her tasks; she is bold in her vision. She doesn't just make things; she multiplies them. Her hands produce, her mind plans, and her efforts expand beyond her home into the lives of others.

Today, the call to be driven isn't about burnout or overachievement. It is about showing up with passion and persistence for the things God has placed in your hands. Whether you lead a business, care for a home, write stories, or support a team, your work is sacred when it is done with intention. Driven women don't just get things done; they build, shape, and release what is within them for the good of others.

To live in her image is to rise with purpose, work with vision, and give your best to reflect who God is. Purpose-driven work becomes worship when it flows from love and intention.

In His Image

God, as Creator, reveals the heart behind being driven. In the beginning, He designed each day of creation with purpose and rhythm—bringing light, land, life, and rest in perfect order. Nothing was rushed, and nothing was random. Everything He made had a place and a purpose.

Being driven in the image of God means approaching our work the way He did. His work created beauty, function, and flourishing, and ours can too. When we embrace our assignments with care and consistency, we echo the creative drive of the One who formed us.

Our productivity isn't for performance but to participate in what God is doing in the world. Driven work becomes worship when it reflects the heart of the Creator.

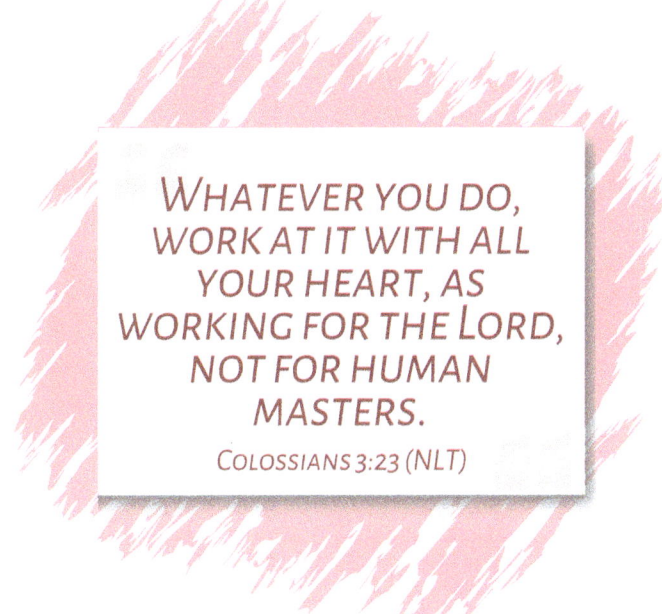

> WHATEVER YOU DO, WORK AT IT WITH ALL YOUR HEART, AS WORKING FOR THE LORD, NOT FOR HUMAN MASTERS.
>
> COLOSSIANS 3:23 (NLT)

THINK ABOUT IT

What kind of work brings you the most fulfillment? Why do you think that is?

_____
_____
_____
_____
_____
_____
_____

Do you approach your responsibilities with drive or dread? What might need to shift?

_____
_____
_____
_____
_____
_____
_____

LIVE THIS TODAY
I am driven by purpose, not pressure.

Identify one area of your life where you've felt uninspired or stuck. Write down a specific action you can take today to reignite purpose in that area. Then, commit to one step that reflects excellence, vision, and intention.

_____

_____

_____

_____

_____

_____

_____

_____

_____

_____

_____

_____

_____

_____

NOTES

Dignified

She is clothed with strength and dignity; she can laugh at the days to come.

Proverbs 31:25

IN HER WALK

Proverbs 31:25 reveals a woman who carries herself with unwavering inner strength and dignity. Life's uncertainties do not easily shake her; instead, she faces the future with confidence and joy. The strength she wears speaks of resilience, courage, and the ability to stand firm in the face of challenges. Dignity, paired with this strength, gives her calm assurance. She doesn't panic about tomorrow because her character has been shaped by purpose, wisdom, and trust.

In the ancient world, dignity was often tied to external status or societal roles. But the Proverbs 31 woman teaches us that dignity begins within. It is not about perfection or public applause; it is about knowing your worth and living with intention. Her strength enables her to stand firm through life's storms, and her dignity keeps her anchored in truth. Together, these two qualities form a powerful presence, enabling her to navigate life with courage, grace, and a steady heart.

Today, we are invited to live the same way. In a world that often praises hustle over health and performance over peace, dignity reminds us that our value is not defined by what we do but by who we are and how we carry ourselves through what we face. It is a quiet resistance to fear and insecurity. Dignity radiates confidence from the inside out.

Strength and dignity are not outward appearances but inward postures, shaping how we face the future with courage and peace.

In His Image

God, as Love, reflects perfect strength and dignified grace. His love is steadfast and deeply rooted in who He is. Throughout Scripture, we see a God who remains faithful in every season, offering comfort and courage to His people. He lifts the humble, honors the brokenhearted, and leads with quiet authority.

To live in her image is to reflect that same divine love through our dignity. Just as God's love does not waver, our identity remains secure in Him. We are not defined by our achievements or failures but by the One who calls us beloved. When we walk in this truth, our confidence aligns with heaven.

Dignity becomes more than how we carry ourselves; it becomes a reflection of the God who carries us. True dignity is rooted not in what we do but in who He is.

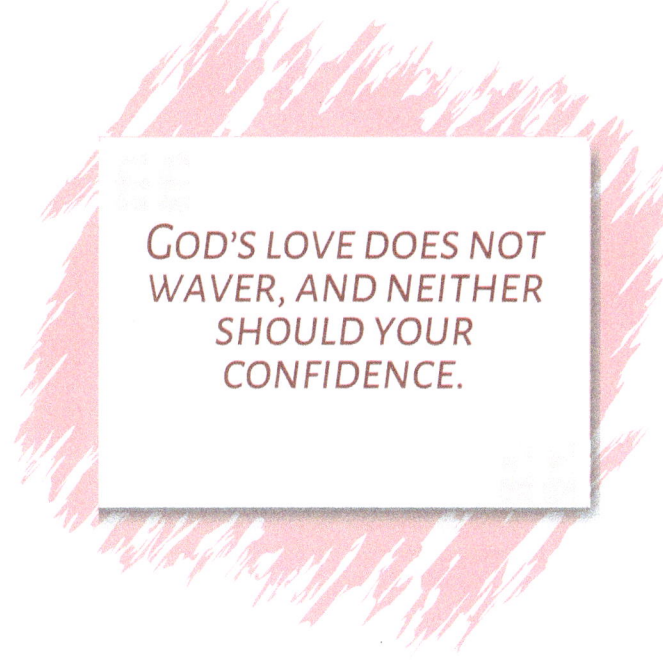

God's love does not waver, and neither should your confidence.

Think About It

What does dignity mean to you and where have you seen it modeled well?

_____

_____

_____

_____

_____

In what situations do you find it difficult to walk in strength and confidence? Why?

_____

_____

_____

_____

_____

_____

LIVE THIS TODAY

Dignity is quiet strength rooted in trust.

Write about a situation you are currently facing with uncertainty. How can you clothe yourself in dignity by trusting God's love as you walk through it? Then, choose one way to reflect His strength in your posture, tone, or attitude today.

_____

_____

_____

_____

_____

_____

_____

_____

_____

_____

_____

_____

_____

_____

_____

NOTES

Hopeful

She is clothed with strength and dignity; she can laugh at the days to come.

Proverbs 31:25

IN HER WALK

The second half of Proverbs 31:25 gives us a striking image: a woman who meets the future with laughter. This is not shallow optimism or blind denial; it is a quiet, powerful hope that comes from deep within—a confidence rooted in something greater than circumstances. She is not overwhelmed by the unknown or paralyzed by anxiety. Instead, she lives from a place of trust and clarity, able to smile at what lies ahead.

This kind of hope is rare and radiant. It does not ignore hard things but stands strong in the middle of them. Her laughter is an act of faith—a declaration that her heart is secure no matter what tomorrow brings. Why? Because she knows who holds the future. Her days are built on faithfulness, wisdom, and trust in God, so fear does not get the final say.

Hope like this is hard to manufacture on our own. It grows as we spend time with God, let go of control, and anchor ourselves in His promises. The world may tempt us to brace for the worst or obsess over "what ifs," but this woman shows us another way: face the future with joy.

Her laughter teaches us that joy is not the absence of hardship but the result of hope. Her confidence does not come from perfect plans but from a perfect God. When we live this way, we invite others to rest and rejoice as well.

You do not need to have it all figured out to laugh at what lies ahead; you only need to know that God is already there, and He is good. Joy is possible because God is present in every tomorrow.

In His Image

God, as Light, shines brightest when life feels darkest. For those weighed down by uncertainty, sorrow, or fear, His light breaks through with unwavering hope. Scripture tells us, "The light shines in the darkness, and the darkness has not overcome it" (John 1:5). This is why the Proverbs 31 woman can laugh at the days to come: even when the future is unclear, God's light illuminates her path.

Light reveals truth, and truth assures us that God is faithful. His promises are sure, His presence steady. When we fix our eyes on Him, even shadows lose their power. Hope rises, not because the darkness disappears but because His light never does.

To live in her image is to reflect this joy-filled confidence and to rejoice not in what we see but in the One who sees all and leads us forward with radiant, unshakable hope. True joy is not found in knowing the future but in trusting the God who holds it.

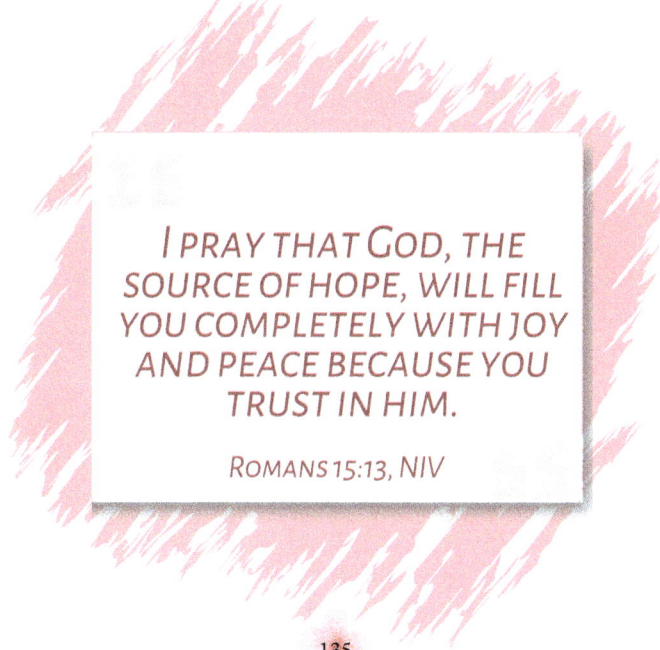

I PRAY THAT GOD, THE SOURCE OF HOPE, WILL FILL YOU COMPLETELY WITH JOY AND PEACE BECAUSE YOU TRUST IN HIM.

ROMANS 15:13, NIV

Think About It

When you picture your future, do you feel dread or hope? Why?

_____
_____
_____
_____
_____
_____
_____

What would it look like to laugh at the days to come with confidence in God's light?

_____
_____
_____
_____
_____
_____
_____

LIVE THIS TODAY

Let your joy be proof that you walk in the light of hope.

Write down one fear or uncertainty you are carrying. Then, find and write a truth from Scripture that speaks directly into that place. Post it somewhere you will see it often, and speak it over yourself every day.

NOTES

WISE

She speaks with wisdom, and faithful instruction is on her tongue.

Proverbs 31:26

IN HER WALK

The Proverbs 31 woman is not only known for who she is and what she does, but also for what she says and how she says it. Her words are wrapped in wisdom, and her instruction is faithful, reliable, and rooted in truth. This verse reminds us that wisdom is not just about knowing the right thing; it is about applying what we know with grace, discernment, and purpose.

Her wisdom flows from a life aligned with God. She does not speak to impress or prove herself, but to build others up and offer guidance that brings clarity and peace. Her words carry weight because they are born of prayer, experience, and integrity.

In ancient Hebrew culture, a woman of wisdom was deeply valued, especially one who taught with kindness. This woman's words did not cut down; they lifted up. She carried herself with spiritual maturity and emotional discernment, creating an atmosphere of peace around her.

In today's noisy world, it is tempting to speak quickly, respond emotionally, or share without thinking. But a wise woman slows down. She listens well. She does not strive to be the loudest voice, but the most anchored one. Wisdom teaches us when to speak, what to say, and how to say it with love.

You do not need to have all the answers to walk in wisdom. You only need a heart that seeks God, a posture of humility, and the courage to use your words to build rather than break. Let your voice be a reflection of the light within you.

IN HIS IMAGE

God, as Light, reveals truth and grants wisdom that brings clarity in confusion. His Word illuminates our path, showing us the way we should go. Divine wisdom is pure, peace-loving, and unwavering, just like the God who gives it.

To live in her image is to reflect that same light through our words and decisions. When we lean into God's wisdom, we become steady voices in a world of noise—beacons of truth that guide others toward Him.

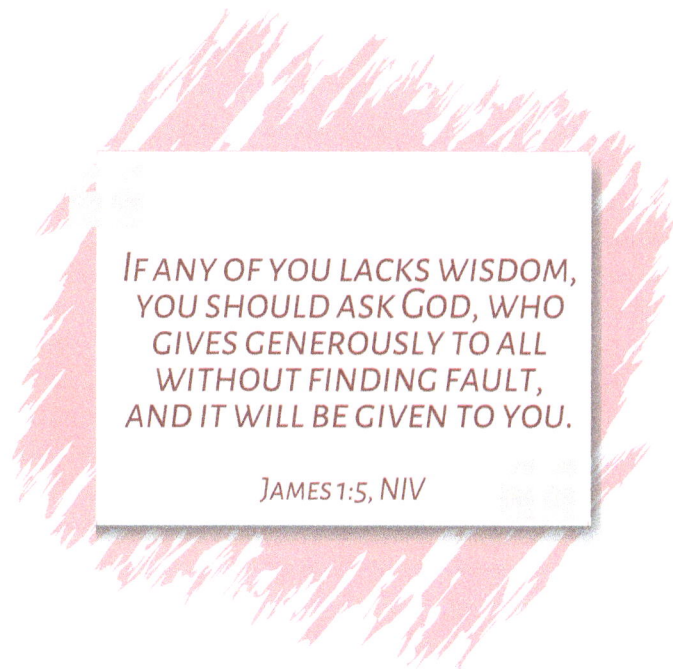

If any of you lacks wisdom, you should ask God, who gives generously to all without finding fault, and it will be given to you.

James 1:5, NIV

THINK ABOUT IT

What areas of your life do you feel most confident in offering wise counsel and which areas do you still struggle?

_____
_____
_____
_____
_____
_____
_____

When was the last time your words brought peace or clarity to someone? How did it feel?

_____
_____
_____
_____
_____
_____
_____

LIVE THIS TODAY

Let wisdom guide your voice and grace guard your words.

Write down one area of your life where you want to grow in wisdom. Then, plan two specific ways you will seek God's guidance in that area this week—through study, mentorship, prayer, or another intentional practice. Write them down and commit to follow through.

NOTES

Intentional

She speaks with wisdom, and faithful instruction is on her tongue.

Proverbs 31:26

IN HER WALK

The words of this woman are filled with wisdom and faithful instruction, the evidence of a voice shaped by experience, understanding, and love. Her speech isn't reactive; it is thoughtful and purposeful. She chooses her words with care, knowing they hold the power to build up or tear down.

In her image, we are reminded that what we say matters. An intentional voice reflects maturity, self-awareness, and a desire to serve others. This woman communicates wisdom in a way that nurtures trust and encourages growth. She speaks truth with grace, offering guidance that brings peace rather than confusion.

Wisdom is more than knowledge. It is the ability to apply understanding with skill. In ancient culture, scribes and sages were honored not for how much they knew, but for how faithfully they lived it. The Proverbs 31 woman reflects this truth. Her words are not idle chatter but faithful instruction, cultivated through spiritual maturity and intentional living.

In our world of instant replies and constant noise, the call to be intentional with our speech is radical. Whether speaking to loved ones, sharing online, or making decisions in leadership, we have the opportunity to pause and speak from a place aligned with God's heart. Our words can guide or mislead, soothe or provoke, heal or harm.

To be intentional means to listen first, to ask God for wisdom, to think before we speak, and to make space for grace in our tone. When we choose intentionality in our words, we carry the weight of wisdom with humility, and in doing so, we build a legacy of peace.

IN HIS IMAGE

God, as Father, speaks with unmatched intentionality. His words never return empty; they create, restore, and guide. From the beginning of time, when He spoke light into darkness, to the whisper of His Spirit that comforts us today, God's voice has always been purposeful.

Scripture is filled with examples of God speaking at just the right time and with just the right tone. Whether offering correction, comfort, or commission, He never reacts in haste. His words are deliberate, redemptive, and powerful enough to shape both history and hearts.

To live in her image is to echo the Father's intentional voice. Just as God speaks from a place of love, wisdom, and clarity, we are called to reflect His nature in the way we communicate. Our words, when offered with intention, can bring life and truth to others, becoming a small but faithful echo of the Father's instruction.

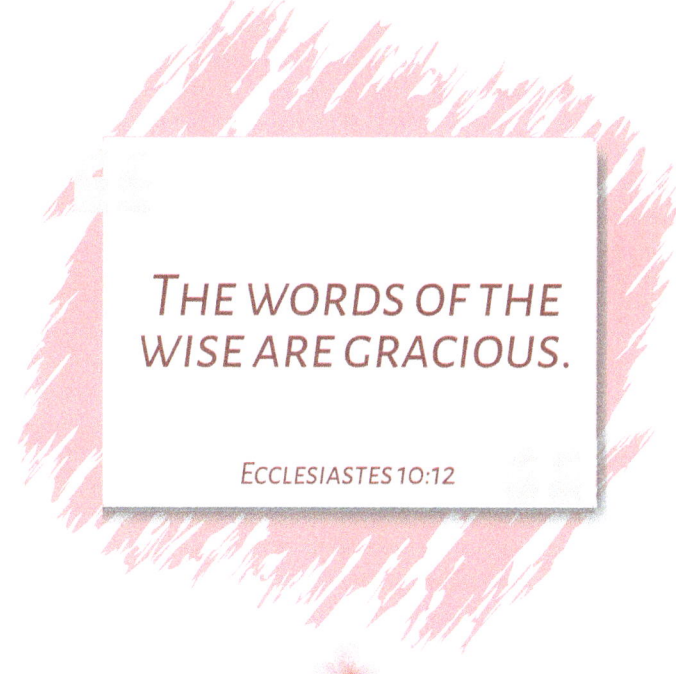

THE WORDS OF THE WISE ARE GRACIOUS.

ECCLESIASTES 10:12

THINK ABOUT IT

When was the last time your words brought peace or clarity to someone?

_____
_____
_____
_____
_____
_____
_____

Are there areas in your life where you speak without intentionality? What would it look like to pause before responding?

_____
_____
_____
_____
_____
_____
_____

LIVE THIS TODAY

Let intentionality guide your tone, timing, and words.

Practice intentional speech today by pausing to take a breath before you respond in conversations. Ask the Holy Spirit to guide both your tone and your timing. Write down one situation where you often react quickly, and plan how you will approach it differently with wisdom.

NOTES

Attentive

She watches over the affairs of her household and does not eat the bread of idleness.

Proverbs 31:27

IN HER WALK

Today's verse presents this woman as not only active but also attentive. She watches over her home out of love, care, and responsibility. She is present, she notices, and she responds. By being tuned in to what is happening around her, she creates an atmosphere where peace can dwell.

The Hebrew phrase "watches over" carries the idea of keeping guard or preserving. Instead of standing at the door with a weapon, she guards with wisdom, prayer, discernment, and compassion. Her leadership flows from her willingness to be fully present—not just physically, but emotionally and spiritually. She is not idle or checked out. She is engaged, discerning what is needed, and offering herself with grace.

In a distracted world, attentiveness feels countercultural. It is easy to default to busyness or numbness and to go through the motions while missing what truly matters. This verse reminds us that attentiveness is sacred. When we tune in to our homes, relationships, and responsibilities with love, we reflect the heart of a God who sees, knows, and responds.

Being attentive means pausing to listen, noticing subtle needs before they become crises, and stewarding your space, your people, and your presence with care. The Proverbs 31 woman challenges us to be present where it counts. When we are, we create environments of safety, strength, and trust.

In His Image

God, as our Father, is the ultimate example of attentiveness. Scripture tells us that He neither slumbers nor sleeps (Psalm 121:4). He watches over His children with relentless care, aware of every detail, attuned to every cry, and present in every moment. His attention is not limited by time or space. He sees us fully and loves us faithfully.

To live in her image is to reflect that divine attentiveness. Just as God watches over us, we are called to notice, nurture, and respond to the needs around us. His attentiveness is not controlling; it is compassionate. When we live with that kind of awareness, we create space for healing, peace, and purpose to take root.

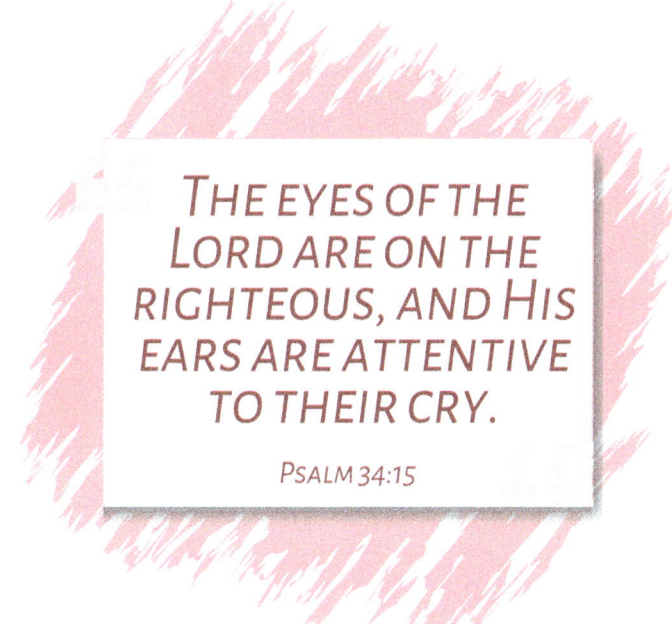

> *The eyes of the Lord are on the righteous, and His ears are attentive to their cry.*
>
> Psalm 34:15

THINK ABOUT IT

In what areas of your life have you been present in body, but not in heart or attention?

_____
_____
_____
_____
_____
_____
_____

Who in your life might need you to show up with greater awareness, empathy, or responsiveness?

_____
_____
_____
_____
_____
_____
_____

LIVE THIS TODAY

Attentiveness cultivates peace when we are present.

Pick one relationship or area of responsibility in your life where you've felt distracted or disengaged. Choose one intentional action to show up fully today—whether it's listening deeply, offering support, or simply being present without your phone or agenda.

_____

_____

_____

_____

_____

_____

_____

_____

_____

_____

_____

_____

_____

NOTES

Legacy

Her children arise and call her blessed; her husband also, and he praises her.

Proverbs 31:28

IN HER WALK

In Proverbs 31:28, we see the quiet reward of a life well lived. The Proverbs 31 woman does not chase recognition, yet her family cannot help but honor her. Her children rise and call her blessed. Her husband praises her. These words are not flattery; they are the fruit of years sown in love, integrity, and presence. Her legacy flows not only from her actions but also from the atmosphere she created.

This verse reminds us that legacy is not something we leave behind after we are gone; it is something we cultivate with every choice, every word, and every act of love. It is found in the daily rhythms of listening with empathy, showing up when it is hard, speaking life over our loved ones, and creating safe spaces for others to grow. The Proverbs 31 woman teaches us that true influence is shaped in the ordinary moments.

Legacy is about presence—showing up with grace and intention, even when no one is watching. We may not always see immediate fruit, but our faithfulness is sowing seeds that will blossom in time. Love matters. Consistency matters. The way we nurture and invest in others shapes stories that will outlive us.

Today, reflect on the kind of legacy you are building—not only through accomplishments, but through character. You do not need a platform to make an impact. You only need a heart that loves well and a life that reflects God's faithfulness. Like the Proverbs 31 woman, quiet obedience and daily devotion create a ripple effect that speaks of blessing, honor, and the goodness of God for generations to come.

IN HIS IMAGE

God, as Love, is the architect of eternal legacy. His love shapes generations, transforms hearts, and never fades. Throughout Scripture, we see how God's covenant love builds not only nations but also families. His faithfulness to Abraham created a legacy that stretched far beyond his lifetime. His compassion toward Israel, His mercy in Christ, and His Spirit within us all reveal a God whose love leaves an indelible mark on those who encounter Him.

To live in her image is to reflect this enduring love in our relationships. Like God, we are invited to lead with compassion, speak with truth, and serve with grace. Legacy is born when our love mirrors His.

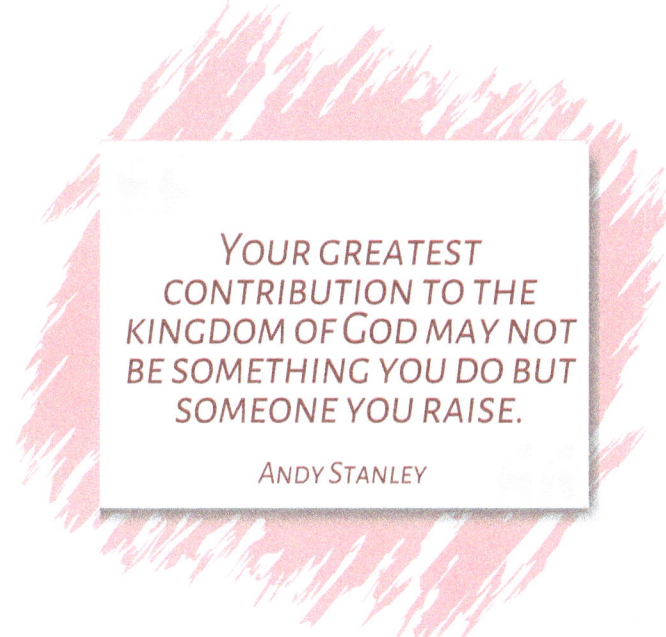

YOUR GREATEST CONTRIBUTION TO THE KINGDOM OF GOD MAY NOT BE SOMETHING YOU DO BUT SOMEONE YOU RAISE.

ANDY STANLEY

Think About It

What kind of legacy do you hope to leave in your family, friendships, or community?

___

___

___

___

___

___

___

Are there consistent habits or words you want to cultivate to reflect God's love more fully?

___

___

___

___

___

___

___

LIVE THIS TODAY
Legacy is not left—it is lived.

Identify one relationship where you can intentionally invest legacy-building love. Write a note, give your full attention, or affirm someone's value in a lasting way.

NOTES

Exceptional

Many women do noble things, but you surpass them all.

Proverbs 31:29

IN HER WALK

What sets the Proverbs 31 woman apart is not a life of perfection, but a life lived with intentional excellence. While many do noble things, she surpasses them because she gives her best from wholehearted devotion. Her character, consistency, and love are what elevate her. She is exceptional because she shows up with courage, grace, and faithfulness day after day.

This verse is not about comparison, but about distinction. She is not better than others because she competes harder or performs more. She stands out because she lives aligned with her calling, offering her time, energy, and love with humility and purpose. Her excellence is measured not by achievements but by the lives touched through her care, wisdom, and enduring strength.

In a world that often chases applause or burns out in the pursuit of doing it all, the Proverbs 31 woman reminds us that being exceptional is not about being everything to everyone. It is about being faithful to who God created you to be. It is about walking in your lane with integrity, cultivating your gifts, and honoring your assignment with joy.

She teaches us that greatness is found in faithfulness. Her family rises to call her blessed, not because she sought praise, but because her love and consistency changed their lives.

Today, let this verse remind you that your consistency matters, and your quiet sacrifices matter. Faithfulness in the ordinary is building something extraordinary. As you live in alignment with God's heart, you reflect the kind of exceptional beauty that inspires honor, love, and legacy.

In His Image

God, as Creator, models excellence. From the grandeur of the stars to the intricate design of a single cell, His work is intentional, breathtaking, and full of meaning. He did not just create a functional world; He created one bursting with beauty, purpose, and delight.

Everything He does is marked by excellence—not for the sake of perfectionism, but because love does not cut corners. God's creativity is generous, and His attention to detail reflects a heart that longs for connection, flourishing, and joy.

To live in her image is to reflect this same excellence in how we live and love. Like God, we are invited to pour intentionality into our work, relationships, and service. When we give our best, no matter how small the task, we mirror the Creator who always gives His best to us.

> *The most extraordinary lives are built in ordinary faithfulness.*

THINK ABOUT IT

What does "exceptional" look like in your life?

_____
_____
_____
_____
_____
_____
_____

Are there areas where God is inviting you to offer your best, not for perfection, but for purpose?

_____
_____
_____
_____
_____
_____
_____

LIVE THIS TODAY

Excellence shines when love and purpose meet.

What is one daily habit, role, or responsibility where you can show up with more purpose and intention this week?
Write down a plan for how you'll pursue excellence; not for perfection, but as an act of love and faithfulness.

_____
_____
_____
_____
_____
_____
_____
_____
_____
_____
_____
_____
_____
_____
_____

NOTES

DEVOTED

Charm is deceptive, and beauty is fleeting; but a woman who fears the Lord is to be praised.

Proverbs 31:30

IN HER WALK

This verse brings the focus back to what truly matters. While charm and beauty may capture attention for a moment, they are not the foundation of a meaningful life. The Proverbs 31 woman is not praised for her appearance or eloquence, but for her devotion to God. Her reverence and relationship with Him give her life depth, influence, and lasting impact.

To "fear the Lord" is not about living in terror. It reflects deep awe, love, and respect. It is a life shaped by surrender, obedience, and trust. The Proverbs 31 woman is guided by God's wisdom, anchored in His truth, and strengthened by His presence.

This verse calls us back to what endures. Devotion to God does not fade; it deepens with time. It transforms how we see ourselves, how we treat others, and how we respond to the world around us.

To live devoted is to live anchored. It means choosing to prioritize God's voice over the world's noise. It is waking each day with a heart that says, "I am Yours." A woman who fears the Lord radiates something eternal. She draws others in, not because of charm or beauty, but because her life points to something greater.

Devotion is not flashy, but it is powerful. When you live with devotion, you walk with a steady confidence that comes from knowing who you are and whose you are. That is a life truly worthy of praise.

IN HIS IMAGE

God, as Judge, sees beyond appearances. He looks at the heart—the inner posture of devotion, surrender, and truth. Throughout Scripture, we are reminded that God delights not in outward rituals but in hearts that sincerely seek Him.

He honors those who walk humbly with Him, who choose obedience over popularity, and faithfulness over fleeting praise. As our Judge, He is righteous and loving, not harsh. He rewards those who live with integrity and devotion.

To live in her image is to reflect God's view of what truly matters. We align with His values when we honor Him above all else. Devotion becomes the lens through which we live, lead, and love, trusting that He sees, He knows, and He honors the posture of our hearts.

THE LORD DOES NOT LOOK AT THE THINGS PEOPLE LOOK AT. PEOPLE LOOK AT THE OUTWARD APPEARANCE, BUT THE LORD LOOKS AT THE HEART.

1 SAMUEL 16:7, NIV

Think About It

In what areas of your life have you been more focused on outer appearance than inner devotion?

_____

_____

_____

_____

_____

_____

What does fearing the Lord look like in your everyday life?

_____

_____

_____

_____

_____

_____

LIVE THIS TODAY

Devotion is revealed in a heart that honors God above all else.

Write a short prayer of devotion to God. Use this as a declaration of your desire to put Him first in every area of your life; from your thoughts and relationships to your work and decisions.

_____

_____

_____

_____

_____

_____

_____

_____

_____

_____

_____

_____

_____

_____

NOTES

Humble

Charm is deceptive, and beauty is fleeting; but a woman who fears the Lord is to be praised.

Proverbs 31:30

IN HER WALK

Yesterday, we explored what it means to be devoted. Today, we take that devotion one step further by focusing on humility: the quiet strength that flows from knowing who God is and who we are in Him.

Proverbs 31:30 reminds us that charm and beauty, while appreciated, are temporary. What endures is a heart that fears the Lord. This woman does not rely on outward appearances or social recognition to define her worth. Her strength is rooted in her surrender. Her life shines because she lives humbly, not from insecurity, but from a deep understanding that all she has and all she is flows from God.

In today's culture, humility is often mistaken for weakness or self-doubt. Biblical humility is neither. It is strength wrapped in surrender and confidence clothed in grace. It allows us to serve without needing credit, to lead without arrogance, and to love without demanding anything in return.

A humble woman does not shrink back from her gifts, because she knows they are not for her glory. She walks confidently in her calling while pointing back to the One who called her. Her humility makes space for others to grow, feel safe, and encounter love without judgment.

As we close in on the final days of this devotional, let this be a moment to reflect on how humility shapes the way you lead, love, and serve. True beauty, the kind that lasts, is not loud. It is gentle, steady, and secure in the presence of God.

In His Image

God, as Love, reveals the beauty of humility through Jesus. Though fully divine, Jesus came in human form not to dominate, but to serve. He washed feet, welcomed outcasts, and laid down His life to rescue ours. His humility was not a sign of weakness but of divine strength clothed in compassion.

To live in her image is to reflect that same love. We are not called to shrink but to shine in a way that points others back to God. When we live with humble hearts, we make room for God's presence to flow through us and bring healing, honor, and hope to those around us.

Humility is not thinking less of yourself, but thinking of yourself less.

— C.S. Lewis

THINK ABOUT IT

In what areas of your life do you feel the pull to prove your worth?

_____
_____
_____
_____
_____
_____
_____

How does humility shift your perspective in leadership, relationships, or decision-making?

_____
_____
_____
_____
_____
_____
_____

LIVE THIS TODAY

True beauty flows from a humble heart surrendered to God.

Choose one way to serve quietly today without seeking recognition or approval. Journal how it made you feel and how it reflected God's love to others.

NOTES

Honorable

Honor her for all that her hands have done, and let her works bring her praise at the city gate.

Proverbs 31:31

IN HER WALK

We have journeyed together through 30 days of exploring the heart, character, and calling of the Proverbs 31 woman. Today, we arrive at the final verse, and it brings everything together in a powerful declaration of honor.

Proverbs 31:31 is not only a compliment; it is a commissioning. It recognizes the value of a life well lived—one marked by faithfulness, purpose, sacrifice, and love. The woman described here does not demand praise; she simply lives with intention, and her life speaks for itself. Her work, both seen and unseen, carries weight. Because she has poured herself out with joy and diligence, she is honored publicly.

This verse reminds us that honor is not a fleeting pat on the back but a lasting testimony. It is the legacy of consistent love, resilient faith, and unwavering integrity. The kind of honor described here is not reserved for the famous or flawless; it is for the woman who chooses, day after day, to show up, to build, to serve, and to love.

It is for you.

You have walked through days of self-reflection, growth, conviction, and encouragement. Now you are invited to embrace the truth that your life, when rooted in God, is honorable. Every whispered prayer, act of love, and sacrifice made with joy matter.

As we close this journey, let these words settle deep in your spirit: your hands have done good work. Your life tells a story of grace and grit. Your voice, your presence, and your impact all deserve honor.

So keep walking. Keep building. Keep living in His image. What you are doing, who you are becoming, and how you are showing up have an impact on the world.

IN HIS IMAGE

God, as Judge, sees what others often miss. He weighs the heart and honors what is eternal. Unlike the world, which exalts performance, God celebrates surrender and faithfulness. His honor is not reserved for the loudest or most visible, but for those who align with His heart—for those who build homes of peace, live lives of love, and steward their days with sacred intention.

To live in her image is to reflect the righteous nature of God and to live in such a way that even when no one else is looking, He sees and He honors. He has promised that those who are faithful with little will be entrusted with more, and those who walk in integrity will never be overlooked in His kingdom.

Honor is God's gift to those who walk closely with Him, not as a reward for perfection, but as recognition of a heart fully devoted to Him.

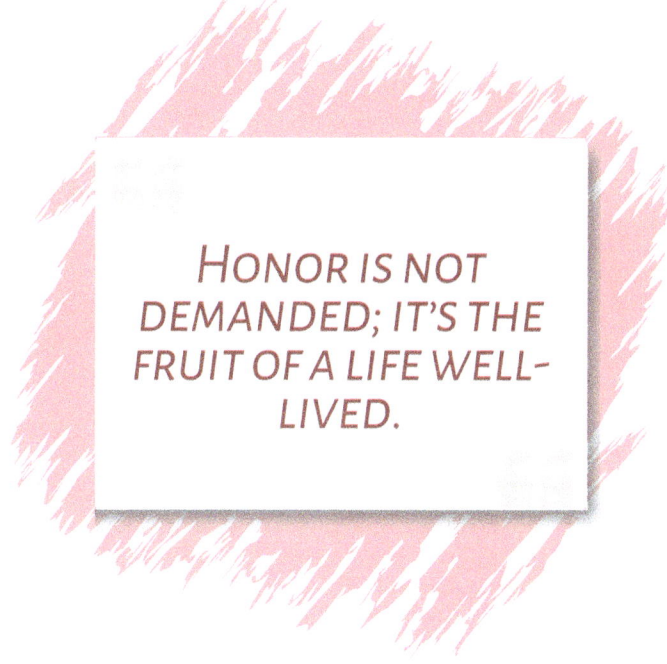

HONOR IS NOT DEMANDED; IT'S THE FRUIT OF A LIFE WELL-LIVED.

Think About It

How have you seen the fruit of your faithfulness show up in ways that brought quiet honor?

_____
_____
_____
_____
_____
_____
_____

What does living an "honorable" life look like for you in your current season?

_____
_____
_____
_____
_____
_____
_____

LIVE THIS TODAY
Honor is the echo of faithful love.

Write down three specific ways you've grown over the past 31 days. Celebrate what God has cultivated in you and take one step today to walk in that growth with confidence.

NOTES

The Journey Continues

If you have made it here—through all 31 days—pause and take a breath. Let this moment settle.

You did more than read a devotional. You chose to show up each day and meet God in the quiet places. You reflected, wrestled, prayed, and paid attention to who you are and who He is. That matters.

This journey was never about perfection. It was about becoming. And the truth is, you are still becoming.

In Her Image is not a list of tasks to perform; it is a mirror that reminds you of who you already are: a woman made in the image of God. Strong. Wise. Compassionate. Purposeful. Resilient. Loved.

My prayer is that these days stirred something in you. That you found language for your strength and permission for your softness. That you saw how your story is sacred, your work is holy, and your presence matters more than you realize.

But do not stop here.

Return to the pages that challenged you. Journal what you are still processing. Share your favorite day with a friend. Read In His Image to deepen the foundation. Join our community and stay connected. And above all, keep walking in alignment with who God created you to be.

You are a reflection of His heart.

You are a ripple of His love.

And the world needs what is inside you.

With much love,

Andrea

About Andrea

AAndrea John is a teacher, speaker, and the director of Ripple, an equipping center formerly known as Jesus House. She is passionate about helping women uncover their identity, discover their purpose, and walk confidently into their destiny.

Andrea is the author of The Journey, In His Image, and Breaking Free, and a contributor to Paper Crowns Volume 1. Her writing blends biblical insight with personal vulnerability, inviting women to exchange pressure for peace and perfectionism for purpose. She also hosts the Destiny Awaits Podcast, where faith, identity, and purpose remain at the center of every conversation.

To continue the journey beyond these pages, connect with Andrea and explore more resources at www.andreajohn.com.

Want to Lead a Group or Host a Gathering?

If *In Her Image* has impacted your life and you're feeling called to share this journey with others—whether through a book club, small group, women's ministry, or retreat—I would be honored to walk alongside you.

This devotional was created not just for personal reflection, but for community. Women grow stronger when we grow together.

If you're:
- Interested in leading a group
- Looking for bulk orders at a discounted rate
- Planning a women's event or retreat
- Wanting to invite me to speak, teach, or host a session with your group

Please reach out. I would love to support you with resources, encouragement, and next steps.

Contact Me:
Visit AndreaJohn.com or email me directly at hello@andreajohn.com

Together, we're raising up women who live in His image and it starts one gathering at a time.

Let's create a ripple effect of identity, purpose, and destiny.

Other Books by
ANDREA

IN HIS IMAGE
DISCOVER YOUR TRUE IDENTITY

Discover your true identity by exploring God's nature, empowering you to embrace your purpose and step into your destiny

BREAKING FREE
A STORY OF HOPE, COURAGE, AND SURVIVAL FROM ABUSE

A powerful novella about a woman's courageous journey to escape an abusive marriage and rebuild her life for the sake of her daughters.

THE JOURNEY
EXPLORE, DISCOVER, AND EXPERIENCE LOVE

An interactive Bible study designed to guide you through Scripture, worship, and personal reflection, helping you encounter God's transformative love and step into your divine purpose.

AVAILABLE ON amazon

Have you read Volume 1?

- 8 Accounts of God encounters that will **ignite your hope** and **build your faith**
- 8 Activations to help you **experience God's presence** in your everyday life
- 8 Amazing authors that are ready to serve you and help you **connect with the transforming love of God**

Do you have a story that can change the lives of others?

Your light needs to be seen.

JOIN THE  Family

Our Membership includes:

- ✓ Full access to our growing Training Library to help you write, publish, and promote your book

- ✓ Weekly Group Coaching

- ✓ Marketing Support

- ✓ Community & Accountability

- ✓ 25% discount on 1:1 Coaching

- ✓ 25% discount on Publishing Packages

You are the light of the world.
We're here to help you shine.

www.papercrownmedia.com/subscribetoday

www.ingramcontent.com/pod-product-compliance
Lightning Source LLC
Chambersburg PA
CBHW061230070526
44584CB00030B/4063